BEGINNING at home

the liturgical press

MARY PERKINS

author

BEGINNING at home

the challenge of christian parenthood

emerson and arleen hynes
discussion topics

virginia broderick
artist

Beginning at Home is one item in the "Popular Liturgical Library," a series of publications on the sacraments, sacramentals, holy Mass, liturgical year, Divine Office, family life, etc. Full information will be sent upon request. Address: The Liturgical Press, St. John's Abbey, Collegeville, Minnesota.

Nihil obstat: William G. Heidt, O.S.B., S.T.D., *Censor deputatus*. *Imprimi potest*: + Baldwin Dworschak, O.S.B., Abbot, St. John's Abbey. *Imprimatur*: + Peter W. Bartholome, D.D., Bishop of St. Cloud. February 22, 1955.

dedicated to the holy family-joseph, mary, jesus-in whose home the divine ideal of family life found perfect fulfillment

contents

POPULAR
LITURGICAL
LIBRARY

study questions
and discussion
topics follow
each chapter

1 the christian pattern

Along what lines should we try to educate our children? How much of modern civilization should we try to bring them up to accept, how much to reject, how much to reform? How best can we train them for whatever God may want them to do for Him in the unknown world of the future?

Before one is actually immersed in the task of parenthood, the answers to such questions seem fairly simple. "Bring up children along traditional Christian lines . . ." "Train them in Christian principles . . ." But when one is faced with the innumerable decisions of daily family life, it does not seem so easy always to determine the "traditional Christian lines" of child training, or to see what "Christian principles" could or should be applied in actual practice.

How much, for example, should you let small boys follow the current local fashions in clothes? in toy pistols? in candy and gum? If you let them be as much like "everybody" as your means permit, short of anything obviously sinful or leading to sin, will you be giving the children the best preparation for not being like "everybody" in things that would be sinful? What is the line and where should you draw it?

In other times, society as a whole guided parents in such "drawing of lines" and it also backed up their authority with its own. There was an accepted way of going about the business of living, there were customs and conventions, there was a definite social pattern which was at least remotely Christian. Parents could usually count on the help of the community in which they lived in giving their children some Christian standards of individual and social behavior.

But today there are few "communities," in the old sense of the word. There are no true social patterns, there are few customs and conventions that will help us in the art of Christian living. We must try to communicate to our children the Christian way of looking at life, the Christian way of dealing with life.

And we must do so while we are living in the midst of a society not exactly opposed to our "point of view" (as an agnostic would call it), but so confused in its own outlook that it confuses us, making it very difficult for us to hold our own point of view clearly or to act in accordance with it consistently. We have to incarnate a Christian way of living in our homes in the midst of a society neither Christian nor truly pagan but secular, that is, disconnected from the influence of God or of "the gods," so far as that is possible.

The Christian culture which we parents must fashion in our homes day by day, then, needs to be at once strong and supple, definite and adaptable. For it must train our children to live as Christians both at home and outside the home, both now and in their future lives.

But how can we best go about such a task? If we tackle it like a picture puzzle, taking pieces of advice even from the most authoritative sources and trying to fit them together, we may find only a puzzle as a result. Unless we ourselves have some blueprint, some master-plan by which to judge whether to adopt Father A's scheme of family prayer, or Sister B's, whether to follow Psychologist X or the equally eminent and Catholic Psychiatrist Y in his ideas on child discipline, we shall let ourselves in for much bewilderment and little Christian peace.

But we do not have to look far to find such a master-plan. We have it right before our eyes in God's own plan for bringing up all His children "in Christ." As we all know, God's method of education is sacramental; He uses visible and tangible things to bring us to the knowledge and love of the invisible; He teaches us how to use our human powers of body and soul, how to use the visible creatures of His universe in His worship and in His service.

He Himself is the great "Sacrament," the visible image of the invisible God, who has made Himself our way and our truth and our life. It is by living a visible human life, by doing a man's work, by suffering and dying as men suffer and die, that He wrought the work of our redemption. And it is in a visible Church, His Body, that He prolongs and fulfills His work through the centuries.

In the life of the Church, Christ teaches us Divine truth through human teachers, by means of human words, in images and stories taken from the visible world and from ordinary human experience. He pours out on us His own life and powers by means of the sacraments and sacramentals, conforming the force and pattern of our lives to His.

These, again, are administered to us by other human beings; their grace reaches us under sacramental signs of visible things and audible, comprehensible words. And we are taught to respond to Him by prayer of our human voices and imaginations and minds and wills to take our part in His work, by loving and serving Him with our human energy and skill as He dwells in our visible fellow human beings. And, finally, summing up our whole lives and the purpose of our lives, we take our part in the visible sacramental sacrifice of the Mass.

God's master-plan, then, is to be found in the work of Christ our Lord Himself, God and Man, His work of redeeming mankind. And our education of our children should surely proceed along these same lines if it is to be truly Christian education. We should make it as far as lies in our power a *sacramental* education, following and fitting into God's own plan.

We should try to teach the children the invisible truths of the faith by means of the visible things around us, by means of the visible actions of daily life; we should try to give them the habit of seeing all created things as, in some way or other, *signs* of the power and wisdom and love of God. We should try to train the children to make the thoughts and words and actions of daily life true signs of their love of God, able to be offered with our Lord's sacrifice in the Mass.

Such a plan of education may seem very obvious and trite until we begin to think out some of its possible implications. For example: as things are, most of us think we have done everything possible to sanctify our family meals by the three-times-a-day effort to say grace. But suppose that we began to follow out the sacramental implications of our family meals . . .

In the holy Eucharist, Christ's own body and blood, His life and His grace, our gift of ourselves together in Him to God, and God's gift of Himself to us, are all made present under the *signs* of bread and wine, human food and drink. And, as modern scholars tell us, the basic design of the Mass is that of a Jewish family meal. Our family meals, then, are meant to teach us and our children about the banquet of the holy Eucharist. Our food and family meals are meant to be the humble human reflections of the sacred meal of the holy Eucharist, which itself is a reflection of the eternal feast of heaven.

In the light of these facts, imagine a meal which the father earned by a piece of "sharp business" in which he did somebody out of the price of a day's food; a meal consisting of food which the mother obtained by pushing in ahead of ten other people for a bargain at the supermarket; which she prepared in a temper and shoved onto an untidy and not-too-clean table; food which looked like something else and contained virtually no real nourishment; a meal to which the children come completely unwashed, knocking each other over in their hurry; a meal eaten in uncharitable silence, or to the accompaniment of mother's complaints about the neighbors.

Such a meal obviously bears no relation at all to the Table of God. It is not a *sign* capable of teaching the children anything about God's banquet. It will certainly give them no notion at all of why heaven should be compared to a feast. Such a meal is a completely secular activity, un-Christian, hardly even human.

But think of the possibilities inherent in our family lives if both the bread-winner and the bread-maker were trying to make each meal and everything connected with it more and more fit to be a humble human *sign* and reflection of the banquet of the holy Eucharist. The cooking and preparation of meals, the day-by-day, year-by-year, often seemingly hopeless task of training the children to cleanliness and decent table manners would take on real purpose and point, and so would the even more long-drawn-out and difficult job of training them to happy and interesting and charitable table conversation.

Let us suppose, for instance, that the price of the meal is earned by the father's running a small hardware store as a real neighborhood service, making available to his neighbors at just prices the things they need for daily living; or, for that matter, by any other honest job that in some way honestly contributes to human welfare. Suppose that the mother bought the materials for the meal from a neighborhood grocery and vegetable store, the owner of which was also trying, according to his lights, to serve his neighborhood rather than make a fortune.

Suppose, further, that the mother, letting the children help her as much as their age and ability allowed, did her best, with whatever real food the family could afford, to prepare a meal that would both nourish her family and please them. Suppose that she served it carefully and lovingly; that the children acted, not like little angels, but like little Christians-in-the-making, with standards of hand-washing, orderly eating and Christian behavior that they did not always live up to, but were at least aware of.

Suppose, too, that an attempt was made really to pray grace before and after the meal; that the conversation at the meal was taken part in by everyone, according to his age, that the children were learning to attend to each other's mental and spiritual needs for interest, love and attention, and to each other's physical needs for salt or butter. Such a meal would be a truly Christian family meal, a real *sign* in its own order, of the eucharistic banquet.

No matter if such an occasion were to look and sound much like any other family meal where small children are present—a more or less messy affair, with the children occasionally spilling things, using their fingers instead of their forks, interrupting the parents' conversation in spite of rebuke, and the parents occasionally becoming short-tempered in the effort to eat and educate at the same time.

None of this would affect the main point, that the parents are trying as best they can, in the light of the sacramental significance of the holy Eucharist, to align everything concerned with their daily bread toward the requirements of full and fruitful participation in that banquet which is the sign and pledge of the everlasting wedding-feast of heaven. (In any case, God Himself has made the material *signs* of heavenly realities necessarily crude and, in a sense, unworthy of those realities, so that we would take them as signs and signs only and not as the realities themselves. St. Thomas points out that Holy Scripture uses crude rather than 'noble' things as the basis for its figures and metaphors for this same reason. We parents, then, have no need to be ashamed of the crudity of our living picture-language, our daily family life in all its messiness, awkwardness, seeming confusion and lack of perfection. For if we are trying to order all its elements in the light of what marriage signifies—the union of Christ and the Church, and toward our all achieving that union through our daily family lives—then, surely, we have the 'one thing necessary.')

Trying, then, to think and act along such "sacramental" lines should begin to give us some real standard by which to judge the food we buy (and some real reason to make it worth the trouble of growing it ourselves when possible); by which to decide how and where to buy it; by which to see how best we can spend our time and energy in preparing it . . . and so on.

Now suppose that many families were to try to act in such a way. What vast areas of human life would, slowly, begin to be restored in Christ! And our children, trained in such sacramental thinking, would grow up, with God's help, to be far ahead of their parents in thus seeing and judging our whole commercial system, our whole way of life, in the light of Christ and in knowing how best to go about acting in and for that light in the foggy world of today.[1]

And here, surely, is the proper task of the Christian laity —to sacramentalize daily human living and all the materials and actions and occupations bound up with it. Priests "mediate" between us and God; they bring us the grace of Christ in the sacraments, the sacramentals, by their prayer, and they offer us to God with Christ in the Mass. And we, the *laos,* the people of God, are, analogously, to "mediate" between the mystical Body of Christ and the un-Christened world of men and things. We are to help to bring not only our own children, but also our non-Catholic neighbors to Baptism, to Christ.

We are to build the houses that the priest will bless, and live in them in the power of that blessing. We are to take days and weeks and years and re-order them to that pattern of holy human living that the liturgy of the Church lays out. We are to work in all the rightfully human occupations of

---

[1] Needless, perhaps, to say, the ideal of fully Christened family life is not that of monastic life. St. Benedict modelled the monastic family on the Christian family, but that does not mean that the Christian family should try to pattern its life on that of a monastery. For the monastery is designed to lead its members to Christian perfection, to *"run* in the road of God's commandments," but the family has to start its members on the road to Christian perfection and teach them to *walk.* The ideal family meal, for instance (I speak as one less wise), should normally include conversation, for part of the children's training in Christian eating is to learn how courteously and happily to share experiences and ideas while courteously sharing physical food. By such complete human "sharing" we fashion our kind of sign and reflection of the eucharistic feast. The monastic meal, on the other hand, is conducted in silence or with spiritual reading, so as to unite the monks' minds on the highest possible level, leading them through the "sign" of the meal to thoughts of the reality. But the monastic meal presupposes many years of training in family meals, otherwise it would seem (at least to the mother of small boys) that the participants would distract each other from God, rather than lead one another to Him in their common act of dining!

modern living and re-order them and all the material things they involve, to the life and service of Christ's members, and so to the glory of God. And thus we shall be doing our own part in re-establishing all things in Christ, in extending that consecration of the world which our Lord inaugurated by His coming.

It is not easy, of course, to see how many of the fields of modern human life can best be sacramentalized—how some of them can be sacramentalized at all. But it is not so hard to see how home life can be made more Christian and more "Christening," for here we are dealing with the comparatively simple fundamental facts of human life: eating, sleeping, dressing, housework, play.

If we parents begin here, as well as we can, with the light and grace of Christ, we shall see more clearly as we go along what can be done in our immediate neighborhoods. We shall see how best to unite our own brains and influence in Catholic family action of one sort or another. We shall begin to see how to extend the influence of Christ into streets and stores, farms and factories.

If we train our children to sacramental thinking, in sacramental living, we shall, certainly, be educating them along truly traditional Christian lines. Moreover, children so educated should be able to see, far more clearly than we do now, how modern life can and may be made holy, re-oriented to Christ. So we shall be training them both for their next ride in a street-car, and for their future work for Christ. And so we shall be giving ourselves, here and now, the plan, the norm, we need for judging the applicability of good specialist advice to our particular needs, and for making the innumerable small decisions of daily family life.

Let us, then, take some of the elements of daily life that have been made to seem most secular by the spirit of our times, and consider how we can best go about the work of re-storing them in Christ, of integrating them into a truly Christian home life, and a truly Christian home education.

First of all, human beings. These have been thought about and written about and discussed from so many un-religious angles that we need, perhaps, to begin by re-thinking out the implications of the fact that our children and ourselves and all our fellow human beings are primarily children of God, redeemed by Christ, made to share in His work on earth and in His glory forever in heaven.

Next, things and places. We need to think out once more and explicitly what is the truly Christian attitude towards these.

That work also has been divorced from any connection with God's plans or providence is all too obvious as soon as we think of the ways in which the majority of modern men spend the greater part of their working lives. And from the general consent of Christians to this state of affairs comes the un-Christian idea that only the special chosen few who are priests and religious 'have a vocation'—the rest of God's people just 'have jobs.'

These elements of our ordinary lives, then, we will consider in the chapters of this book, not because they include every phase of life, or because considering them goes to make up a complete program of education, but because they are the elements which seem to need explicit re-integration into the whole plan of Christian life and into the full joy of Christian living, if we are to begin in our homes to restore all things in Christ.

Discussion topics

1. What can be done to awaken children to the spiritual significance of food and of meals? What methods can be recommended for getting children to come to meals on time and to be orderly during meals?

2. How often should religious topics be introduced during family meal conversation? Who should lead the prayers before and after meals?

3. Discuss the meaning of the phrase, "sacramentalizing daily human living." To what extent do we succeed in achieving this ideal in our own American community, and in what ways do we fail?

4. Is it possible to sacramentalize one's individual family life without first changing the general environment in which the family lives?

5. Does the approach of the author seem too idealistic to be practical in our busy modern world? How does one determine what is "practical"?

1. Why is it more difficult today than it was fifty years ago for parents to follow a "Christian pattern" in rearing children?

2. What is the meaning of the statement that "God's method of education is sacramental"?

3. What is the difference in the part played by the mother, by the father, and by the children in preparing a truly Christian meal?

4. What are some of the differences between a monastic family meal and a Christian family meal?

5. What is the function of the laity in a secular world?

2 OUR NEIGHBORS

We believe, of course, that every human being is, in one way or another, a *sign* of God his Creator and Sanctifier and of Christ his Redeemer. We ourselves, incorporated into Christ by Baptism, are meant in God's plan to become more and more Christ-ened all our lives long, increasingly perfect undimmed *signs* of Christ, through whom He can love and serve His Father and His brethren. And He has so identified Himself with the human race that we can recognize and serve Him in every person we meet, baptized or not, sinners or saints.

Every human being is made by God, called to share God's life in Christ, and, therefore, actually or potentially a child of God, a brother, co-worker and co-heir with Christ, a temple and instrument of the Holy Spirit. We are, in fact, to be judged as fit for heaven or not, on the basis of whether we have treated other people as *signs* of Christ Our Lord: "Come, blessed of My Father—when *I* was hungry, you fed Me . . ."

There is no need to go into details as to how this *sacramentality,* this sacredness of each human being, should affect our own actions, and our family life in general. We are all accustomed to try to act in the light of these truths. But we must now consider some of their implications in education.

On the side of self-development, each child is meant to become another Christ in his own individual way. Surely, then, all the long process of caring for his needs, physical, mental, and spiritual, and of training him to take over his own care and development, can and should be ordered to this high purpose. And surely, also, the truths that God has told us about human nature will afford us a guide as to how to order all our training to this purpose of forming 'other Christs.'

The children, as they are given to us, are, first of all, *signs* of God their Creator; they are God's creatures, made to His image and likeness. Their bodies and souls and all their powers are then fundamentally good, planned by God to be used for good. Consequently, as the children become aware of their own bodies and of their physical prowess and powers, we can teach them to reverence and admire God's workmanship, and to want to cooperate with God's purposes.

When the children want to know, for instance, what happens to the food they eat, we can tell them the basic scientific facts in simple language, and lead them to praise the Maker of these marvels. We can also lead them to see the reasons for eating proper food, for taking reasonable care of their health so as to cooperate with His plans.

Such a habit of mind fostered all during childhood should likewise prepare the children for a real appreciation of our remaking in Christ. These bodies, so wonderfully made to begin with, have been re-made by Baptism, Confirmation, the reception of the holy Eucharist, to be Christ's own members, the temples and instruments of the Holy Spirit. And if we should use them and develop them properly because they were made by God, how much more since He has given them this added wonder and sacredness.

In the same way, as the children come to be aware of their own emotions, and of their own spiritual powers, we can teach them what God actually intended these powers for—that Tommy's explosiveness, for instance, was given him by God to be harnessed as a driving force to help him overcome obstacles in doing God's Will. He has to learn to control this power with God's help, but in itself it is as good and necessary as is the explosive power of gasoline in making a motor run. And, along the same lines, we can show the children gradually what the graces of the sacraments do, and will do to bring all their powers to perfection.

But our children are, as is only too evident, fallen children of Adam, even as we are. (If anyone of us did not believe in original sin, surely the experience of being a parent would soon convince him of its truth, so evident are its effects not only on the children but on ourselves!) Even when God's life has been given us in Baptism, even with the grace of the sacraments, we all still have weak wills, tending to sin, uncertain minds, tending to error, emotions tending to run away with us rather than work for us.

But our incorporation into Christ by Baptism means that we can share in His victory over sin, sinfulness, and the devil who would lead us into sin. By the grace of His Passion and Cross, even our weakness and our tendency to sin can work for our good and His glory. We can be brought in His strength to the glory of His Resurrection.

As the children, then, become aware of their own weaknesses, of their own tendencies to sin and sinfulness; as they begin to realize how much easier it is to do the wrong thing, or the less good thing than the right one, we can try to show

15

them that all this is no cause for surprise or undue alarm or worry. Every human being has these tendencies because of Adam's sin; they can somehow, in God's love, finally work for our greater happiness; our job is to try to accept the hazards of our special weaknesses patiently, to ask God's help in overcoming them; to realize that overcoming them perfectly is a long, long job, but that God has promised the victory if we hope in Him and keep on trying.

But any parent who tries to teach the children self-control and self-discipline and to deal with their faults along these lines, soon discovers that it involves a great deal of discipline for him (or her) also. We find that we have to discard those handy parental weapons of "How could you . . .!", "To think that a child of mine . . .!", "Well, I am surprised!" Why in the world should we, fallen children of Adam ourselves with all our own so evident failings, have any right to be so surprised that our children take after us also in having faults? Yet it is a rare parent who has never said something similar!

And we have to discard also those other easy lines of attack, "Where is your self-respect . . .?", "What will people think?—", and try to work instead along the lines of respect for God's making and re-making, recourse to God's help and His love, the desire to carry out His plans and do His work.

Again, the effort to direct all our teaching and training of the children along these lines soon shows us the reasons for positive discipline and training. We see that we not only have to try to keep our tempers with the children—which is hard enough, God knows!—but that, on the other hand, we have no right simply to make ourselves the servants of their impulses and whims.

We see that we need to learn to serve Christ in each child, not by giving in to him in his various phases of growing up, but by helping him to develop the raw material of his nature into the image of Christ that God intends him to become. We have to make ourselves the intelligent servant of his true needs as a Christian-in-the-making, and this includes the need for discipline and necessary punishment as well as for positive training in obedience, self-control, and self-development.

There is, of course, no hard and fast line between the individual and social development of a child; for to develop oneself is to develop one's possibilities of serving others; to develop skills in serving others is to develop oneself. And, in general, it seems that most children find the idea of self-perfection a rather static and unappealing motive, whereas the idea of fitting oneself both by discipline and development to be someone's fellow-worker, therefore to help Christ to win His victory, build up His Kingdom, help other people come to His happiness—all this makes good sense.

It would seem better, therefore, both for supernatural and obviously utilitarian reasons, to consider the child's personal, individual development as only one aspect of the whole process of his growth as an interdependent member of the mystical Body of Christ.

But with regard to what is usually called "social adjustment" as such, we can begin, as soon as a child is becoming aware of other people as people, to show him that they are sacred because they are God's, and related to himself in that sacredness because he is God's also.

A small child is aware of himself as a maker—of block houses, mud pies, sand castles, peggy-toy guns, etc.—before he is explicitly aware of himself as a child in relation to his parents, and long before he is explicitly aware of himself as a person.

He can be taught very early, then, to realize that people are things that God made with special love and care for very

17

special reasons, things that He wants us to learn to treat properly and to use as He meant them to be used. "God gave Johnny a dark skin and you a lighter one. . . . Wasn't He clever to think up such a lot of different ways of making people!" "You know you didn't like it when Tommy knocked down the house you built; well, God doesn't like it when you knock Tommy down, because He made Tommy. . . ."

Soon the children can also begin to realize and act upon the implications of the fact that people are not only things that God specially made, but also His children that He specially loves. They can learn that all children are brothers and sisters of God's Son who became a human child like themselves. They can learn that some of us already have the great privilege of belonging to His special family, the Church. "Bobby is so nice because God made him that way. . . . You look a little like Daddy, don't you? Well, all God's children look something like Him, and that's one reason why we love them." "You wouldn't let anybody hit little sister while you were around. Well, we all ought to feel the same way about everybody in the world, because God has made them all our Lord's brothers and sisters and ours too."

As the children begin to be aware of other people's failings and weaknesses and failures, we can show them here also that mistakes and faults and sins are nothing to be surprised at, that only God is perfect and always to be counted on; that people are to be loved and cared for and served even though they are not perfect, since God made them and loves them and redeemed them and wants their company in heaven forever.

So we should help the children as they grow up not to become "disillusioned" by any fact that they learn about human nature or by any experience that they may have of other people's weakness and sinfulness. We should help them

18

to be properly on their guard against other people's weaknesses as well as their own, while at the same time hoping for the best from other people as being redeemed in Christ together with themselves.

In the light of the full Christian truth, we can also show the children, as they become increasingly aware of their own reactions to other people and of theirs to them, that true affection, friendship and love are reflections of God's own love, and that they mean wishing and working for the other's true good, ultimately for his Christ-likeness on earth and his eternal happiness in heaven. We can help them to see in the mystery of true human attractiveness and lovableness, a shadow and sign of the infinite attractiveness of God, a sign that is meant to lead us beyond itself to Him.

So we can help them to begin to watch their own motives in their loving and giving, to learn to love and give for the sake of the other person, and, ultimately for Christ, rather than for the sake of making themselves feel good or excited. We can help them to judge whether another person's affection is real, and therefore leading them toward God, or false and leading them away from Him; and so with their own feelings for others. And with God's help, we can give them some sort of real chart to guide them toward God and the Christlike service of others amidst all the surprise, pain, bewilderment, comfort and happiness involved in their future relations with other human beings.

Such a "sacramental" way of looking at our children and their development will, incidentally, make more endurable the inescapable drudgery involved in caring for small children, and even more, the almost sickening effort often required by the disciplining and training of children in the essential habits and basic skills of ordinary human life.

And such a "sacramental" way of looking at themselves

and their neighbors should make it much more interesting to the children to take over the work of their own self-discipline, of keeping up and developing their own good habits, physical, mental and spiritual. Such things as remembering to brush one's teeth twice a day, to keep one's clothes reasonably clean and neat, to make oneself reasonably attractive, to eat real food rather than candy and ice cream, etc., can be shown as jobs to be done for God, part of taking proper care of His instrument, His temple, one's own body.

In the same way, we can show the children that learning how to choose their own reading or movies or television shows, to study lessons thoroughly, to control their daydreams, all such things, are part of their responsibility to God for taking proper care of the member of Christ, the instrument of the Holy Spirit that God wants each child to become. And, again, we can teach them that learning how to sweep a floor or read a book thoroughly, how to cook, how to drive a nail, how to do arithmetic, are not simply tiresome necessities, but are part of their present or future service of Christ in others.

This does not mean, of course, that whenever mother tells Suzie to sit up straight, she must always add "because God's child oughtn't to slouch"; or that whenever father stops Tommy from beating up his little brother, Tommy should be reminded that "Johnny is God's child too." Such a course would be likely to turn its victims away from all religion! But it does mean that we parents should keep before our own eyes the sacramental vision of what people are and are meant to become, that we try to act upon it ourselves, and that we communicate it in words to the children as their interest, curiosity or special needs give us the opportunity.

In other words, we should try to think and act ourselves, to teach the children to think and to act, in such a way that the explicit doctrinal teaching about what human nature is and is meant to become, as the children learn it in formal religious instruction, will be merely the formulation of truths already to some degree realized and acted upon.

None of our training, of course, can substitute for the children's own free wills. We cannot save them without their own consent—God Himself does not do that. We cannot force them to become saints, nor even passably good Christians. All this is, ultimately, up to God's grace and their own freedom; our part here is that of prayer.

But God has entrusted the children's training to us during the years of their growth. We cannot help training them somehow—if only in self-defense. Let us, then, try to train them in accordance with His own plan, for His own plan, not stopping at any lesser plan or purpose. And then surely He will supplement our feeble efforts and help our children to become by His grace, what He Himself wishes them to be.

study questions

1. How will we be judged by God as fit for heaven? (Read aloud the Gospel according to St. Matthew 25: 34-46.)

2. What should we teach our children as being the reason for taking care of our body and for being proud of the body?

3. What importance does the doctrine of original sin have for parents in the task of rearing children?

4. How should children be told about the rights and failings of other people?

5. What is the basic reason for discipline of ourselves and of our children?

22

discussion topics

1. "Each child is meant to become another Christ." How can this idea influence a mother in her daily work of feeding, clothing, and training her children?

2. List the principal failings common to parents in dealing with their children. Show how these defects could be modified by the development of a deeper religious understanding and motivation.

3. Discuss the typical reactions in our community toward peoples of different races, colors, nationalities, and religions. How can we, in our own particular environment, teach our children to practice neighborly love toward members of other groups?

4. What qualities should a "model child" have at the age of 7? at the age of 12? (Would he ever show anger? would he be instantly obedient in all things? would he consciously have a religious motivation for every act? how advanced would he be in awareness of social obligations?)

5. Discuss the extent that parents should regulate their children's recreational interests, and the means that they should use. What responsibility have parents for controlling the time and judging the quality of movies, radio and television programs, and reading materials? Is it sufficient merely to censure what is bad? How can positive Christian standards of judgment regarding recreational outlets be developed in children?

3 " . . . you did it unto me "

But everyone we meet is not a *sign* of Christ in exactly the same way. How, then, can we best help our children to recognize, love, serve and, in turn, be served by Christ our Lord as He comes to them in special ways in special kinds of people?

Let us begin with those of our fellow beings who most directly and objectively represent Christ to us: His priests. How can we best help our children to recognize, reverence, love, and be ready to serve Christ the Priest in every priest they may meet?

To *recognize* Christ the Priest in every priest means to recognize the Mediator between God and man, who teaches God's truth to us, brings God's life to us, leads us to serve and love God and to be happy with him forever.

To *reverence* Christ the Priest in every priest means to honor him as sacred to God, set apart, consecrated and empowered for the holiest work in the world; to honor him for

God's choice of him and for his own correspondence with that choice.

To *love* and be ready to *serve* Christ the Priest means to have our wills in tune with Christ's priestly work, eager to have our priests be truly priests to us. It means being ready to help them *in* their work in whatever form of parish activities or Catholic action they suggest; to help them *for* their work by supporting them, not only with money, but, as we find the opportunity, with all those less tangible forms of assistance that all men need, however exalted their office and station—appreciation, the affection of charity, cooperation, opportunities for due relaxation, and so on.

Obviously, a first necessity here is that priests be made realities in our children's lives. If the priest is little more than a figure up at a distant altar once a week, and a voice in the confessional once a month, the children will have little chance to build up any attitude to the priesthood beyond that of vague respect.

Let us, then, give the children every possible opportunity clearly to see and hear the priest when they attend Mass—there is usually room up in the front of the church when there is any room at all!—to witness baptisms and ask questions about what they see, to be present when the priest comes to our houses to visit someone who is sick, in short, to see their priests as they go about their highest priestly work.

Let us also give our priests every possible encouragement to come to our homes as priests, to bless our houses, give special blessings, to visit the sick, and so on, as much as the size of our parish and circumstances permit. And on such occasions let us try to take our part, and the children with us, in making the correct preparations for the priest's visit, and the right responses to his prayers.

Moreover, if our children are to receive from us any idea

of working under and with their priests in helping to bring about the kingdom of God on earth, we shall have to take part ourselves in whatever form of parish activity and Catholic action our circumstances and talents are best suited for. Then the children will have the chance to see us making practical applications of the distinction between office and person, so necessary in all Catholic life. They will see us striving to exercise that humorous and humble charity which does not blind itself to "Father's" imperfections and foibles, realizing that we have just as many and more ourselves—and that Father is trying to be patient and charitable with us.

Finally, we could try to make it as easy as possible for priests, especially for our own parish priest and his assistants, to visit our homes, and to feel at home there. Every Catholic family should surely pray for the grace of having real friends in the ranks of Christ's priests. There is no simpler, or surer (or more enjoyable) way to give our children the opportunity to know and love and serve Christ in his priests than actually to have priests as honored, loved, and familiar guests in our homes—guests with whom we do not "stand on ceremony," but whom we do treat with the respect due their priesthood; guests in whom we can most obviously care for Christ Himself; guests who will argue with the parents and play with the children, but to whom we all kneel for Christ's blessing at the end of every visit.

If every Catholic home were to do all that it could along such lines as these to make and strengthen the bonds of common interest in God's work, of unselfish helpfulness, of real charity between people and priests, how far-reaching would be the effects on the future generation in vocations to the priesthood, in fruitfulness of the Church's work, in the vitality of the Church's life!

Many of the same general means, obviously, are also to

be used in helping our children to come to honor and to be ready to serve Christ in His religious, to bring them to recognize religious as men and women especially dear to Him, who have undertaken at His call to live explicitly, full-time, and by set rules of life, in that bridal relationship of love and total dedication to God which the rest of us must work towards by far less direct methods.

By personal acquaintance and friendship, common work and interests with religious; by reading, by correspondence, by contributions, however small, to the Propagation of the Faith and to contemplative Orders, and so on, we can try to make the manifold forms of religious life a reality to our children. We can help them to grow in gratitude to all religious and in appreciation of the special part religious take in carrying on the great work of Christ.

In this age of widespread vague knowledge about "depth psychology," many of us parents are continually harassed by fears of what we are doing to our children's present and future psychic set-up, by fears of what our children are going to think about us in future years. Whatever measure of truth there may be in the various theories of psychology current today, it is all too obvious that our children do obtain from our behavior to each other and to them, the material for their primary ideas of, and attitudes toward, authority, parenthood, marriage, fatherly love, motherly love, and married love. And we also realize, all too clearly, that, in spite of our efforts, our own conduct is not a perfect model of fatherhood, motherhood, or marriage.

We do, certainly, believe on faith that God will give us, if we pray and work, the graces necessary to bring up our children. But is there anything that God means us to do besides praying that He will somehow bring our children

27

out all right in spite of the psychic dangers seemingly inherent in family life and childhood among fallen mankind?

Here again the Christian and sacramental pattern is the answer to this most modern need. We parents are, it is true, imperfect as images to our children of God's perfect love, perfect parenthood, perfect authority and care; but we are His images nonetheless, by virtue of our office as Catholic parents. We can, then, in accordance with our children's needs and development lead them to an appreciation of both the positive and negative implications of this fact.

Our love and care are only sketchy pictures of God's love and care. Whatever is good and real and right in them comes from God. As parents, we are instruments of God's love, of His care and His will for the children while they are young, and as such we are meant to have their respect and obedience, as well as their love.

But our imperfections and limitations show that we are not God; that we are not meant to be and do not expect to be the most ultimate term of our children's interest, or respect, or filial love. These should go, and the sooner the better, through us and around us and beyond us to God Himself.

"God loves you even more than Father and Mother do. He had to give you both a Father and a Mother to show you something of how much He loves you, and He gave you our Lady too, His own Son's Mother, to be your Mother in heaven . . ." "He gave Father and Mother the job of taking care of you and bringing you up as He wants, so that you can do great things for Him when you grow up, and be happy with Him forever. That's why we have to tell you not to do things that we know would be bad for you, and to do things we know are good for you, till you are old enough to know what God wants yourself. . . ." "God wants you to obey us now as practice for obeying Him directly when you grow up, just as our Lord obeyed our Lady and St. Joseph when He was a boy on earth. . . ."

And also, when it is clear to the children as well as to us that we have made a mistake or been unjust or lost our tempers, let us use such occasions too, as impersonally as possible, to help to establish our children in the right relationship to God's perfect Fatherhood:

"Yes, Mother was wrong. Isn't it wonderful that God can never make any mistakes, and that He loves you and is taking care of you all the time, whatever happens, and however wrong things seem to be. . . ." "Yes, I lost my temper and I shouldn't have. Daddy and Mother have to try to be good, just as you do. But God never loses His temper, however bad we have been, and as soon as we are sorry He gives us another chance. Let's both tell Him we are sorry and ask Him to help us try again. . . ." "Yes, Mother just didn't understand. Isn't it a good thing that God is never too busy to listen and always understands, and our Lady does too and can help you much more than Mother could. . . ."

By thus using the occasions of daily living to point the children's attention and affection through us to God, we shall be doing a great deal to avoid any evil and unbalancing consequences of our own imperfection as parents and of the children's imperfections as growing human beings. Such a sacramental attitude toward our own parenthood should also help us, with God's grace, to avoid both the danger of over-possessiveness and that of neglect.

It should also help the children to avoid the emotional repressions and complications that arise with trying to think that their parents are perfect when obviously they are not. And, such an attitude should also, with God's help, lay the human foundations for that trustful, truly childlike attitude to God which is the essence of spiritual maturity, that attitude

29

which is so much easier to maintain and develop from childhood on, than to establish for the first time in later life.

In the same "sacramental" way, as our children come to adolescence and to a growing realization of the implications of human love, we can use even the imperfections of our own example to show the children what marriage is and should be. We can help our children to realize that the ideal of marriage, of love, of self-sacrifice, of perfect union, is more true and more real than imperfect human beings; that human imperfections are allowed for in God's plan, and do not spoil or mar the Reality of love and happiness in love for which we all were made. And, in doing so, we do much to establish our children in true Christian realism, to save them from "disillusion," to help them grow straight and unhampered toward fruitful Christian maturity.

We all know the beautiful statement of the truth, *Hospes venit, Christus venit,* "When a guest comes, then Christ comes." What is difficult is to show our children by our daily example that we are always happy to have guests of all kinds, because each of them gives us the opportunity to welcome and serve Christ our Lord. We need to try to be happy, at least with our wills, not only to welcome a beloved friend, or an influential acquaintance, but also the bore who is only going to waste our time, and the salesman whose product we do not want and cannot buy.

In all these people equally, Christ the Guest is asking us for the best hospitality that we can give him under the circumstances—say, ten minutes full attention to the bore, and a human smile and word about the weather to the salesman. For the more that we can so manage to give our best to everyone who comes to our door, the more our children will be prepared to realize that it is the One Christ who is coming under all these various guises.

30

And the other aspect of helping our children to learn true Christian hospitality is, surely, to make it a happy and natural and frequent event in our homes. If the children see that "having company" is a strange, unnatural, infrequent affair, requiring all sorts of elaborate preparations, short tempers and stiffness, they can hardly be taught the theory that we are doing such things to welcome the Christ who loves them. On the other hand, they themselves should take part in a reasonable amount of happy, special preparation for expected guests, and so acquire the habit of doing whatever can best be done to honor Christ as He comes to them in our guests.

The sacramental plan of things gives us also the key as to how to help our children to achieve the truly Christian attitude towards those who suffer and towards suffering itself. Since our Lord endured the suffering of the Cross for our redemption, human suffering possesses an objective dignity of its own from this very fact, whether the sufferer himself realizes it or not. And, from our Lord's own words, we know that it is He whom we serve in trying to help the needs of any human being.

In anyone who is suffering, therefore, we may find Christ Himself in His Passion, giving us here and now the opportunity to care for Him, to wait on Him, to sympathize with Him. For these reasons, personal care of the sick is a privilege; for these reasons, the vocations of doctor and nurse are greatly to be honored. Any serious illness or affliction in the family or the neighborhood or among our friends can offer us the occasion for talking over these facts with the children, and for doing whatever we can to act on them.

On the other hand, suffering itself patiently accepted in union with Christ's sufferings, shares in the value of His suffering and is positively valuable for the eternal salvation of souls. As the practical St. Therese says, to accept suffering in this way (and all forms of hardship, trial, and inconvenience) is, as it were, to earn token money which we can give to our Lord to change into real currency by the value of His sufferings, and to use to ransom souls from sin, to free souls from purgatory, to win graces and blessings for those who need them. When our children have to undergo any severe pain, or disagreeable illness, we can begin to give them such a simple and practical view of the possibilities of suffering, and so teach them how to endure it without self-pity, stoicism or softness, with at least the makings of true Christian heroism.

But, in connection with all these truths, whenever we have occasion to talk with the children about our Lord's sufferings, the value of suffering and so on, we should take great care to bring out the fact that it was original sin and, in its train, the effects of the actual sins of all the generations of men, that are responsible for all human suffering. God the Father does not enjoy seeing us suffer; He did not enjoy seeing His Son suffer. But His wonderful ingenuity, so to speak, by means of the sufferings of Christ has enabled us to make use of all this suffering which we brought upon ourselves, to use it in helping Christ with the very work of effecting our redemption.

All modern techniques of helping the handicapped now use the principle of self-help above everything else; when the children are of an age to appreciate such facts, we can point out how wonderfully and how lovingly, "even to the death on the Cross," God Himself has been using this very principle in the work of our redemption. Even small children can appreciate the thought and skill needed to make use of otherwise useless things, and so to appreciate what Christ has done in His suffering, for our sufferings.

And, of course, we must also show them that no human wisdom can fathom all the aspects of suffering; we can only know that God is infinite Love and infinite Goodness, and that somehow He will bring a greater good, far greater happiness for more people forever in heaven, out of all this seeming evil.

Along the same lines, we can give the children the foundations of a truly Christian attitude toward the handicapped. Any form of physical or mental affliction shares in the objective dignity which our Lord's Passion has conferred on all human suffering. In any form of special consideration or service which a handicapped person may require, we can find a special opportunity of serving our Lord. Moreover, only God knows the degree to which any particular person's particular sufferings or handicaps are of positive value in the great work of the redemption, but we do know that such a person has, at the very least, a special opportunity to help our Lord in a most valuable and difficult way in the work of building up His kingdom.

A person so honored is not, then, to be pitied: for pity implies superiority, and who are we to be superior to Christ? But he is to be sympathized with, as our Lord allows us to sympathize with Him in His Passion. Not, of course that we can expect every handicapped person necessarily to be a saint, (or, for that matter, that any great affliction or hardship will necessarily make us saints!), but that he has been given a special opportunity to become so.

When our children are going to meet, for example, a man who is blind, we should discuss quite frankly with them all the handicaps of blindness, so that the children can begin to sympathize with ("suffer with") their future friend. But we should not end up with "Poor Jack, isn't it dreadful that he is blind!" Rather, "God must think a lot of Jack to give him such a tough thing to bear for Him. That's why it is a great privilege to have Jack with us, and let's try to give him as good a time as we can."

Along the same lines, we can show the children how best to help and serve Christ in the handicapped or needy. Obviously, this will not consist in doing what we would like to do for them, but what will help Christ to live more fully in and through them. In the case of a blind person, again, the greatest kindness is to help him to independence; to let him realize that we accept him as a normal human person. So we need to learn to restrain ourselves from the fussy rushing to his assistance that bolsters up our own cozy feeling of helpfulness, to find out instead what kinds of help are really needed, and to accept help from him in our turn whenever possible.

If we thus try to think out and practice consistently the implications of the truth of Christ's special presence in those of our neighbors with special needs and afflictions, our children may be able to learn from us what true Christian charity means. But if we only try thoughtlessly, spasmodically, and sentimentally to "be kind to" the poor or handicapped, our children will be in danger of contracting that sentimental pity, and fear of all forms of affliction which is the modern caricature of the true Christian attitude.

We need also to try to get across to our children the correlative aspect of these truths which concern their own acceptance of help, of Christian charity in every form. One of our great modern vices is to feel disgraced by any need for help, to feel that we must be able to pay in some immediate and concrete way for everything, even for kindness.

Such an attitude is obviously a barrier to the free flow of the warmth and vitality of mutual charity among the members of Christ's Body. For it is, ultimately, a form of selfishness to try to seize every opportunity of serving Christ in one's neighbor and yet to refuse to others that same opportunity as far as one's own needs are concerned. So St. Thomas says that it is itself an act of charity to receive charity—of course in the proper sense of that wonderful word: love shown in loving service of God and neighbor.

We need, then, to try ourselves to give the example and to teach our children how, graciously and gratefully, to accept help of all sorts as coming, somehow from Christ Himself. Such training begins with the inculcation of the simple "Please" and "Thank you" which curiously is so difficult to make habitual with many children. For such ordinary politeness involves a certain amount of true humility, recognizing that one does need things from other people, but that one does not have a right to anything, and that gratitude is only decent.

We want, of course, to bring the children up to be as properly independent as possible, especially of us, in the sense that they gain the habit of trying first to figure things out for themselves before they ask for advice, and the habit of doing what they can for themselves before they ask for help. But we need also to teach them when and how it is sensible and Christian to ask for advice or help, and to accept it, not as one's due, not as if one had been disgraced by needing it, but simply and gratefully in the spirit of true humility. For the spirit of humility is basically a realistic sense of what we are in relation to God and to each other; and, in relation to each other we are all needy in one way or another; we all need others' help; we all need to give and also to receive.

Only many volumes could begin to cover the whole field of human relations and their wonderful possibilities to the eye of Christian charity. We have to show our children how to be truly neighbors to Christ in the people who are our

35

actual neighbors by physical location in our community and parish; how to be neighbors to Christ in needy and suffering men all over the world, to the holy souls in purgatory, and to all the host of heaven. And we need to show the children also how to accept help themselves gratefully and graciously, as coming somehow from Christ.

But, surely, the sacramental view, the effort to recognize and serve Christ as He comes to us in person, is the Christian key to "human relations" of all kinds. All sound knowledge of how human beings act and re-act, about our bodies and nerves and minds and souls, all rightful "techniques" of dealing with people and helping solve people's problems, all this can thus be ordered to the love and service of Christ in our neighbor. And, if we try to begin at home, we can help our children to form the fundamental habits of true Christian charity, capable of taking up all such modern knowledge and equipment and putting it all to the service of Christ.

◊ i s c u s s i o n topics

1. Discuss the ways in which parents can foster religious vocations among their children. What methods are objectionable?

2. Discuss methods of discipline and of punishment of children in the light of the fact that parents are images of God's perfect love, perfect authority, and perfect providence. What are some practical means of balancing love and justice toward children? How can parents tell if they are too indulgent or too stern? if they are inconsistent and arbitrary?

3. Make applications of the principle: "When a guest comes, then Christ comes." Can this spirit be maintained toward all who come to our front door, including salesmen, baby sitters, neighborhood children, and visiting teenagers? Should we make an attempt to invite people to our homes as guests if we think they need help, although we would prefer our privacy?

4. "It takes as much charity to receive as to give." Explain this statement and show how it applies regarding aid and gifts to us from relatives, friends, and neighbors.

5. Discuss the Christian attitude toward pain and suffering as it affects the lesser ailments of daily life. Should parents complain about their ill health in front of their children? Should they act as though they never had pain or discomfort? Should children be encouraged to put up with pain and suffering? What should be the parents' attitude toward the bumps and pains the children suffer?

1. In what ways does a priest particularly represent Christ?

2. List suggestions for making priests "realities in our children's lives."

3. Since children obtain their ideas about authority and parenthood from their parents, does this mean that parents should act as though they think they are perfect and infallible?

4. What part does original sin play in suffering?

5. What is the Christian attitude toward suffering? toward those who suffer?

4 things

Thinking next over the question of how to help our children to grow up with a "sacramental" attitude toward things proves to be a somewhat startling experience. For when one begins to consider the specifications of this Christian attitude, one realizes with dismay how different it is both from the attitude of previous generations, and also from the modern attitude which is now, unawares, forming our children's views and re-fashioning our own.

The old attitude was one of appreciation of the value and quality of things as satisfying needs, providing luxuries, and laying the ground-work for the "finer things of life." Human prudence, thrift, foresight, carefulness with regard to possessions, were among the highest virtues known to this attitude; wastefulness, prodigality, taking no thought for the morrow, lack of ability to make a living, were considered the worst of vices. God was the source of all blessings, but He only helped those who helped themselves, and solid worldly success was a sign of His approval.

Our own parents and the Christian teachers of all ages have warned us against the danger of this attitude. It encourages selfishness, for it makes it seem a positive duty to amass things for oneself and one's family even at the expense of other people and other families. It leads people to overvalue physical comfort, luxury, as well as "refinement," and either to despise or to envy and over-value the "finer things of life" like music, art, literature. Above all, it leads people to see in earthly possessions the guarantee of security and the reward of right living, as did the rich man in the Bible whom our Lord called a fool.

The basic assumption of the modern attitude, on the other hand, an assumption sanctioned both by modern science and by the existence and operation of the mass-production system, is that things really have no permanent form or value in themselves. The form in which we find any object at the moment is accidental; the thing can be junked tomorrow and turned into something quite different and also much better than what we have now, for "progress" is seeing to it that the products of our civilization are inevitably improving year by year.

There is little use, then, in learning to appreciate anything for itself, in learning to value the quality of anything, taking great care of it, especially as there are in existence millions of other objects just like this one, turned out by the same machines on exactly the same pattern. What we can get out of a thing right now is all that really matters, since, however we treat it, we can either get another, or turn it in for something even more modern and more efficient.

Again, ours is, strictly, a "consumer" civilization, one which literally consumes things, uses them *up*. Science has not yet discovered for practical purposes how to turn everything into everything else—how can we now make use of the component parts of the crude oil consumed in the last twenty years, or the coal, or all the metals in our myriad junk piles?

But we vaguely feel that science either has made such discoveries, or soon will. And so we feel justified in continuing to use up raw materials in making things designed to be used up and discarded in order that people will buy new things and thereby keep the system going. And the system must be kept going, because the mass-production machines which are its focus and its fetish must be kept going or money will be lost, men will be thrown out of work, fewer people will be able to buy, panic and depression will follow soon.

The claims of these machines, in other words, have been allowed to reign supreme over true human welfare, let alone the claims of God. The real criterion of value has now become, not the satisfaction of people's real need or what provides them with real pleasures, even on the sensory level, but rather what people can be persuaded to buy in order to keep the system going. For the real needs, and the desires for legitimate pleasures of ordinary people do not provide the ever-expanding market our system must have in order to keep going.

The only way out then, in times of peace or comparative peace, is continually to "create" new "needs," to persuade people that they need ever-new models of their present possessions as well as new things of whose existence they never dreamed. And the means of persuasion necessarily appeal, not to real human needs (which are, finally, self-limiting[1]), but

[1] We are made to need food, drink, etc., in limited amounts and kinds. Beyond this, nobody can try to obtain extra satisfaction by eating more than so much food, or drinking more than so much drink without finally suffering the immediate and/or long-range effects of over-indulgence, which themselves take away the original appetite and of themselves limit temporarily or perpetually the possibility of continued indulgence—in extreme cases, by causing death. This holds good for all physical satisfactions and also for all true cultural needs, namely, for books, music, the fine arts and, even, for com-

41

to the unlimited and illimitable desires that can be awakened in fallen man by appealing to his emotions through his imagination.

If we contemplate soberly the implications of Fr. Vincent McNabb's statement: "Every act of self-denial stops some wheel from turning," it is startlingly clear that our system could not continue as it is without the deliberate discouragement of self-denial, of Christian trust and detachment; without the deliberate encouragement of anxiety, fear, and of what theologians call the lust of the flesh, the lust of the eyes and the pride of life, that is, of fallen man's inappeasable itch for sensations, for acquiring things and "experiences," for being up-to-date, "hep," just as good as the neighbors, secure, successful, etc.

Again, since things are made primarily to be sold, not to be or to do what they are presumably supposed to be or to do, the practice of good workmanship is, generally, accidental, even where the mass-production system still leaves room for its possibility. Things are not, then, generally made as God intended them to be, *for* somebody's special needs, *out of* the proper materials, *by* an intelligent and skilled workman who knows what he is doing and intends to do it for the love of God and man.

Rather, incalculable quantities of God's inanimate and animate creatures are being misused to provide raw material for junk,[1] and millions of men and women are either not

panionship. We cannot really enjoy more than so much reading, music, etc., and over-indulgence in such pleasure results in a form of mental indigestion which itself, temporarily at least, prevents further enjoyment. But the appetite for "thrills," for more and better gadgets, for being ahead of other people, for "security," "success," etc., can never be satisfied, nor does it bring the obvious punishments of these other forms of over-indulgence, for it exists in imagination only, not in the realities of human nature and human needs.

[1] If this statement seems harsh, just go and wander around a department store, especially its basement.

using or are misusing their human facilities to design, produce and distribute goods which, whatever the individual workers' good motives, actually promote not the common good, but the common ill—increasingly widespread selfishness, pride, covetousness, lust, anger, gluttony, envy, and sloth.

Obviously, then, the modern attitude toward things does not simply contain dangers against which we could warn and fortify our children. It is essentially wrong in itself, for it necessarily fosters intemperance in the acquisition and use of things, false solicitude about imagined "needs," the abuse of human work and of God's materials. It necessarily discourages the Christian spirit of detachment, poverty, and the right use of creatures.[1] If it did not, it would break down.

Yet we and our children have to live, work and trade in this civilization. We cannot transform it over-night. We can only do what we can, in an infinitesimal way, to join with others of like mind, and to begin thinking, studying, praying and working towards such a transformation, and,

[1] This is not to say, of course, that people do not practice these virtues today, only that the whole spirit of the times is against our doing so, and is rendering it more and more difficult.

Nor is this to say that "the machine" is essentially un-Christian. There is no such thing as "the machine," only various kinds of machines, each of which needs to be judged on its own merits and its effect on human living. To quote a vital distinction made by John Julian Ryan in a forthcoming book called *Practical Wisdom,* a machine which is a *powered tool* may certainly be an aid to human and Christian living; a powered tool is one in which the machine provides the power but not the control: the work remains always under the direct control of a man's skill: e.g., a power saw, a dentist's drill, a steam-shovel, a tug-boat. Again, a machine which really saves human drudgery (that is, work that requires no intelligence), even though such a machine performs several successive operations automatically, could also obviously, be a means to human and Christian living, e.g., a washing machine, machines for generating power, preparing crude material. Of course, even with regard to such machines the question would remain to be investigated, whether or not they actually do or do not lessen the total amount of human drudgery

at the same time, help to prepare our children to carry on the transformation according to their future vocations. For this purpose, obviously the first thing to do is to become consciously aware of the Church's whole teaching about creatures and their use, and to try continually to rectify our own attitude by this teaching. Then we will be in a position to communicate the Christian attitude to our children and to prepare them for their life-work in the world.

Where we can best, for our purposes, find the Church's teaching about things and their use, is in Holy Scripture and in the liturgy and in the social encyclicals of the recent Popes. From all these sources, we find, to summarize roughly, the following:

1) God made everything for His glory and to be useful to man.

2) God made all things in wisdom, to the image of His Son, and, ultimately, also for the sake of Christ. The vast diversity of creatures was planned by Him: each thing gives Him glory by being and acting according to the nature He gave it, taking its part in the great harmony of creation and the drama of the history of the whole cosmos.

or distribute it more equally, considering the work involved in procuring raw materials, making the machines that make the machines, the actual manufacture, distribution, sales, etc. And also whether or not such machines use up an undue amount of irreplaceable raw materials.

Again, there is no intrinsic reason why the evils of mass production could not be avoided and better results obtained if, in the production of things which must be exactly alike (parts, small objects like pins, screws, etc., and especially raw materials), the process of manufacture were re-thought out and redistributed to allow a man or team of men to work on whole tasks of producing at least whole parts, using their human brains and skill and powers of cooperation instead of simply minding machines. If the amount of ingenuity that is now spent on "making the system work" were spent on thinking and planning to put true human welfare as planned by God before the "efficiency" of machines, perhaps a truly Christian civilization that used machines properly might, with the help of God, begin to be built. Nobody wants to "put the clock back" in the name of Christ; we want, rather, with all human brains and intelligence and skill, to prepare for the coming of "Him who is to come."

44

3) God gave to man, whom He made in His own image and likeness, a share in his power of making and ordering created things. He made various "raw materials" so that men could re-fashion them in various ways, according to their natures and potentialities, and He gave man the intelligence and potential skill to re-fashion such things. He also gave man the power of "ruling" living and non-living created things, that is, of ordering them. By making and ruling things, man was to perfect his own nature as an individual and social being, and thus fulfil the purpose for which God made him; so to live on earth as to prepare for eternal life in heaven; and, in a sense, to complete and perfect God's creation by acting in the capacity of His vice-regent over it.

4) By the Fall, man handed over to the devil, so far as God permitted, his own over-lordship of material things. This satanic power needs to be exorcised by the power of Christ in order that Christians may be able to use and order things for Christian purposes.

5) But, as all things were first made through the Son, made fundamentally good and holy and given their proper degree of life through Him, so by His redemption they have been, in principle, redeemed from the devil's power so that they can be blessed by Christ and given to us, who have been re-made to His image, to use through Him, with Him, in Him, in the love of the Holy Spirit, for the honor and glory of the Father.

6) God made things to be useful to men in two ways: a) by serving their complex physical, mental, and spiritual needs, individually and socially (the very complexity of these needs forcing men, even on the natural level, to specialize in serving one or another, and to serve each other's needs as well as their own), and thus enabling men to grow up and

live and work together on earth, according to God's plan, and prepare together for eternal life in heaven.

b) Things have been made, and used by God in the course of history, to serve also as signs of spiritual realities, so that in the very use of those material things which necessarily take up so much of our time and energy, we can raise our minds and hearts to God, and to the wonders of our creation, redemption, sanctification and eternal life.

Our Lord's own words, and Christian teaching throughout the ages, add several conclusions to these general principles.[1]

1) God only gives us things and lends us power over them to use them according to their natures, to enable us to live according to our human and Christian nature. We have no right to abuse anything.

2) Material goods have been "lent" by God to all mankind, to serve the good of all mankind through all the ages of its history. We have the right to private property only in so far as such an arrangement enables us more effectively and fully to provide for our own needs and serve those of our neighbor. We have no absolute right to anything, in the sense that we are free to destroy it, or to use it wrongly.

3) We have no right, then, to own or to try to acquire more things than we need to provide for our own needs as individuals or families according to our state of life, and to enable us to satisfy other people's needs according to our own special talents and capabilities. We have no right to anything, in other words, which we cannot really use to help us to take our own part in building up the kingdom of God.

4) Anything we have or acquire beyond this norm

[1] See *Rich and Poor in Christian Tradition*—Writings of many centuries, chosen, translated and introduced by Walter Shewring (Burns Oates, London, 1948).

belongs, in charity if not in justice, to others who do need it or could use it.

5) We shall be judged by our Lord on the last day primarily by how we used material and spiritual goods to satisfy each other's fundamental physical, mental, and spiritual needs; by how we used all these things to serve Christ in our neighbor. Therefore, obviously, one of the most important aspects of Christian education, to put it mildly, must be in the intelligent and skilful and habitual use of material and spiritual goods to serve other people's needs.

6) We are not to be "solicitous" about providing for our own needs, that is, to be at all anxious about it, or to spend any more time and strength on it than necessary. If we seek first the kingdom of God and His justice (that is, if we are trying primarily to take our part according to God's will in building up the kingdom according to our vocation), then God has pledged Himself to provide for our needs (Matt. 6:24-33).

7) If we are thus seeking His kingdom, and yet our physical, mental, or spiritual needs do not seem to be provided for, we can be sure that God sees that we have a greater need to share in the poverty and suffering of His Son in His passion, in order to share in our Lord's work in the special way He has planned for us, become the particular 'images' of Christ that He wants us to become, and share in the special way He intends in His happiness forever in heaven.

Now, if we set side by side the main characteristics of the Christian attitude with those of the "modern," we shall see, perhaps, some ways in which to go about our attempt to establish our children in the Christian attitude, to strengthen them against the "modern" one, and to prepare them to take their parts according to God's will in transforming civilization.

First, the Christian tries to find out, to fit into and to take his part in carrying out God's whole plan for the use of himself and all creatures; while the modern attitude considers everything as man's, if he can make it so by "science," to be used in any way he wants. Our first effort, then, should be by the prayerful reading aloud and study of Holy Scripture and of the blessings of the Church, to make ourselves aware of God's whole plan, and of how material creation is included in it.

And our second effort should be actually to go about using things, as far as possible, according to the Church's plan as outlined in the blessings, and to use the blessings themselves,[1] asking our priests to administer them when possible, and otherwise we ourselves, father or mother, saying the words of the blessings and making the sign of the Cross with holy water.

We need to make a continual effort, then, to establish and maintain ourselves in the Christian attitude. One of the best ways of going about it is to read and study and think about the blessings of the Church and the events in Sacred History to which the blessings, indirectly or directly, refer. Then we should have things blessed, as occasion arises, by a priest. And, lastly, we should try to use things according to God's plan as it is shown to us in the blessings.

For example, if the family is about to acquire a new car, we could take the opportunity to study with the children the Blessing for an automobile. We could read over with them

[1] Inexpensive booklets containing translations of some of the commoner blessings are: *Family Blessings*, by Bernard Strasser, O.S.B. (NCWC, Washington); *Family Sacramentals*, by Walter Sullivan, O.S.B. (Grail, St. Meinrad, Ind.); *With the Blessing of the Church*, by Bishop Schlarman (NCRLC Des Moines); *Lord Bless Us*, by Rev. Harvey Egan (Grail, St. Meinrad, Ind.).

the passage from the *Acts* to which the blessing refers. We could discuss our obligation to drive carefully and so make ourselves worthy of the angels' protection. We could also discuss the idea that every journey we are going to take in the new car is a kind of 'sign' of our whole life's journey to heaven.

Then, when we get the car, we could begin our use of it by driving it to the rectory of our parish and asking our priest to bless it. Again, the occasion of a journey by train or boat or airplane could be used to study the blessings for all these means of transportation. Or, lacking a journey, books about trains or planes, cutting out pictures of them and so on, could be used as the spring-board for interest in and familiarity with, the blessings the Church has provided.[1]

In this connection also, since the Christian tries to find out what God made things to be and do, to praise and thank Him for them, and to use them rightly, we can try to be as conscientious and patient and intelligent as possible in the never-ending task of teaching the children to look at things as they actually are; to appreciate them for what they are, and not for something else; to judge man-made products by how well they imitate God's making in being well-made and in fulfilling the needs they are supposed to fulfill.

Such training will involve, as any parent realizes with dismay, a continuous process of "debunking" what the children are told by advertisers everywhere, including their own friends; such debunking, moreover, needing to be carried out as matter-of-factly, humorously and unheatedly as we can manage. On the positive side, this training will involve training the children's senses, to taste, smell, touch, see, and hear what is before them vividly and discriminately,

[1] An almost indispensable family tool here is Fr. Weller's translation of the Blessings of the Roman Ritual (Vol. III, Bruce).

as the indispensable prerequisite and accompaniment to training the children's powers of appreciation, judgment, self-restraint and proper use with regard to toys and tools, food and clothes, furniture and means of transportation, as well as books, music, and pictures.

Then, since the Christian tries to use things as God meant them to be used, while we are training the children to *appreciate* things rightly, from God's point of view so to speak, we need to be training them to *use* things rightly. Such use involves taking due care of things, using them for what they were meant to be used for and not some other way. It also involves constant care to avoid our great American vice of waste, showing the children that it is foolish and expensive, but still more that it is wrong, for it means not using something for what God meant it for.

Children of bicycle age, for example, can be shown that a really well-built bike, made to fulfill its purpose of carrying somebody swiftly and easily from one place to another, is not necessarily a bicycle with many gears, or complete with glittering accessories, but one whose essential parts are strong, well-designed, well-put-together. The children also can be shown that the right use of a bicycle is to learn first to control it, then to ride it swiftly; but that to misuse it by making the tires squeal, loosening the handlebars and so on, is both silly and wrong, as doing an injustice to the nature of the bicycle.

In all this, we will, of course, be working not only against the children's natural carelessness and destructiveness, as parents have always had to do, but against the whole spirit of the times, the spirit of pretending that one thing is just the same and just as good as another which costs more or is harder to make or obtain (why "butter substitutes," for instance, why not simply "margarine?") and the spirit of acquiring and using things for some entirely irrelevant or non-essential reason or purpose (buying a brand of soap, for example, because you get coupons with it to buy something else, admiring a car ·for its "modern lines," using a college education to "get ahead").

All this training in rightful appreciation and rightful use may often seem unendurably common-sense, old-fashioned and prosaic, as well as difficult. Let us remember, then, that its purpose is not to turn our children out as Horatio Algers or "solid citizens," but rather to give our children as complete a training as we can give them in using the things of this world rightly so as to achieve life eternal for themselves and their fellow-men.

But by far the most important aspect of our training of our children in the right use of things, is to train them in making things, especially in making things for other people's needs; and this for many reasons. First of all, such training in making is education of the whole child, body, mind, and soul, towards perfecting him in the image of God the Creator that God wants him to become.

Secondly, no other training is so efficient in inculcating true appreciation of materials, tools and skill in the products of the workmanship of both God and man. If you have once really tried to make a table, you have an insight into furniture-making and a basis for judging good furniture that no amount of book-learning alone can give. And if you have tried to make a table for the use of someone who really needs it, ° then you have had a full experience of mature craftsmanship.

And, finally, since doing things and performing actions are also forms of making in the widest and truest sense, the children should be trained to "make" a dance, a play, a tidy well-swept room, etc., as well as being trained to make actual things, according to their age and capacity. And a higher reason for all this training in making is that the bread and wine used in holy Mass are artifacts of man's skill; if a person had never made anything, it is much more difficult to show him why and how the bread and wine can stand for us, for our human work, for all we have and do and make and are.

In our encouraging and training of the children to make whatever they can learn to make reasonably well, let us then try as far as possible to lead them to make things that somebody really needs (rather, for instance, than things that are easy and effective to make so that kind grandparents will pretend that they like them). And let us try to show the children by any means our ingenuity may suggest that these products of their making are to be offered to God, with our Lord's offering in the Mass, as their work is to be offered with His work, their very selves with Him.

Obviously, also, if we are to train our children in the Christian appreciation and use of things, we must take as much care to give them, and to see that they learn to make and buy for themselves, things that are well made and well designed, of good materials. How can we invite the children to raise their minds to the true Bread of Life, and their hearts in thanksgiving to God, how can we urge good craftsmanship, if we sit down every day at a table made of some plastic that pretends to look like marble, covered with a plastic cloth intended to look like lace; when on the table is the white bread of commerce that has had some small amount of nourishment "added" to its essential constituents, a breakfast food that amounts to slightly sweetened air, and only nourishes because of the milk and sugar put on it. . . ?

Of course, it is simply not possible for most of us to be perfectly consistent about buying real things today, but we can at least do our best. It would be quite possible for some of us, for example, to find out where the nearest furniture factory is, visit it, and buy the furniture we need unfinished, and perhaps, with slight flaws in it (much more cheaply than we could buy the finished product in a store). Much good furniture is ruined only by the finish which tries to make it look like something other than the original wood it is. In any case, we can make it a habit to look for things that are well-made and not pretending to be other than they are. And we can also point out occasionally our own unavoidable inconsistencies to ourselves and the children.

Another characteristic of the Christian attitude towards things is to enjoy the perfections that God, or man, His image, has put into things—whether or not one actually owns the thing and can profit from or enjoy its use. We can, then, encourage the children to appreciate and rejoice in the qualities of other people's things: gardens, lakes, lovely china or furniture or houses, cars, and achievements.

A third characteristic of the Christian attitude as opposed to the modern is that the Christian sees the use of things as a trust, a "stewardship," to be exercised for the love of Christ, for the good of one's neighbor and the whole mystical Body of Christ. We should, then, when the children want us to buy things for them, or want to buy things for themselves, help them to consider not only the quality and price of the things, but also how it fits into the whole picture of their daily lives as Christians: Can you really use it, or learn to use it rightly? Can and will you take proper care of it? Will it cause unnecessary trouble in the family or among your friends? Can you somehow share or enjoy it with other people?

Obviously, this is a habit of mind to be established, not a puritanical check-list. We and the children need things that are just for fun, need to do things just for fun without always consciously adverting to ultimate significances. But such significances do need to be in the back of our minds, to have been thought out at some time or another, or the fun will cease to be fun and become distraction and escapism.

So, in the same way, for major family purchases at least, we can call the children into consultation: Will this labor-saving device, for example, that we can now afford, actually give us more time and energy to praise God better, to love and serve one another in Christ, to serve our neighbors more effectively? Will this relatively expensive means of entertainment really re-create us, or will it simply wear us out and make us less fit to carry out God's will?

Again, the Christian realizes that he has no right to more things than he can really use. We and our children, then, might well have a yearly examination of conscience on our possessions, perhaps at the beginning of Lent, or perhaps in connection with the Bishop's Thanksgiving clothing drive, or some other special opportunity to give things away.

Should father keep that old dress suit he hasn't been able to get into for twenty years? Should mother keep that old extra coat just in case—when so many people don't even have one? What about those half-worn-out shoes that John says he can't get into? Should we keep them for five years till Tom gets that size? Or give them to somebody who needs shoes now?

Such questions are not always at all easy to answer with due prudence as well as charity, and both virtues have their claims. But it does seem from the lives of the saints as if the Lord preferred us to err on the side of generosity when there is any real doubt as to which virtue should be followed!

Again, we can try to show the children both by example and words that giving is an essential part of living, that actually doing without things in order to be able to give to those in need is a normal Christian thing to do, especially in times of penance, Lent and Ember days.

But, since Christians are not to be solicitous or unduly worried about their needs, while we must encourage the children in habits of prudence, foresight, reasonable budgeting and so on with regard to money and to possible future possessions, let us discourage them in any undue amount of planning, worrying, working to acquire things for themselves, especially things that are simply means to personal recreation.

And, finally, since we are followers of Christ, let us try to realize ourselves and to communicate the realization to our children that we have no "right" to freedom from want, that if we lack even necessities, we are sharing our Lord's Passion to some small extent. Grumbling about a lack of comforts, complaining about having less than our neighbors, about not being able to buy things we want and that other people have, all this is unworthy of soldiers of Christ, to whom hardships, doing without and suffering are not important—so intent should we be on accomplishing our mission, doing our job, taking our part in the battle, looking forward to the final victory of Christ.

1. What does the author mean by the "old attitude" toward things?

2. What does the author mean by the "modern attitude" toward things?

3. What are the principal points from the Church's teaching regarding things and their use?

4. What does the author mean by the "right motive" and the "wrong motive" for buying such things as bicycles and soap?

5. Why is it important for children to make things?

Discussion topics

1. Read the Gospel of St. Matthew 6:25-34. Discuss how this teaching of Christ gives us a guide for determining a Christian attitude toward things. Is a housewife materialistic if she wants an automatic washing machine? if she wants new furniture? if she wants a fur coat? a picture window installed in the living room? Does the parable of Christ mean that parents are not supposed to be "solicitous" about things for their children? Should parents practice thrift? have insurance?

2. Discuss ways and means for increasing the use and the appreciation of blessings of things in the home.

3. What things can and should children make at home? About what percent of their time should children be "making things" as compared with the time they spend "being entertained" by watching others perform? Suggest ways in which the average home could be expanded in opportunities for the children to make useful and functional things.

4. Discuss ways and means for aiding children to increase their respect for property—for clothes, family furnishings, other people's property and community property. At what age should children begin to buy and take care of for themselves the more expensive items of property? What standards should we teach them to employ in buying one item rather than another?

5. Discuss the "proper" amount of things that children should have at the various age levels. Do children get too many toys or get them at too early an age? How might the amount of things children have today affect their idea of "stewardship" of property? Are the amount and value of gifts given at Christmas or for birthdays an aid or hindrance to children for developing a Christian concept of goods?

5 places

The modern attitude toward the universe as a whole, toward our earth, toward places made by God or man is, naturally, as secularist as the current attitude toward individual things and possessions. Few people are brought up to look for the power and wisdom and love of the Creator in His creation; even those scientists who recognize the "great Mathematician" or "the great Architect of the universe" usually do not recognize Him as a Person who is interested in mankind. To the majority of people today, the heavens do not declare God's glory, but only man's littleness and impotence; the wonders of heaven and earth do not invite them to praise, but to a pagan sense of *lacrimae rerum,* the tragic fragility and passingness of all things, or still worse, to a kind of wondering despair at the purposelessness and chanciness of nature in all her manifestations.

As St. Bonaventure says, creation was meant to be for mankind a great book in which we could learn about God. Civilizations other than ours have realized in the main that this book was made to mean something, even if they did not know the alphabet or the language. Ours, alas, is the first to hold, as a general assumption of ordinary people, that it is only a meaningless scrawl or, at best, a cold-blooded mathematical report.

We need to arm our children against this assumption as they will meet it in their friends, in popular magazines, in literature, and even in education. We want to equip them not only to possess, but to share with other people the true vision of creation. The sense of the presence of God in His universe which we try to give them must, therefore, be full and deep and mature, rooted in faith and knowledge as well as the sense of awe and wonder native to unspoiled childhood.

Our aim, then, is to give the children a positive sense that the heavens are telling the glory of God. We want to give them the habit of going from "When I consider the work of Thy hands, the moon and the stars that Thou hast set up . . ." to the mystery of "What is man that Thou art mindful of him," a mystery not of doubt that God could be mindful, but of wondering love that He *is* mindful, even to making His only Son the Head and Redeemer of mankind.

We want the children to come to appreciate all the wonders of nature as signs of God's creative power, wisdom and love, and of His redemptive and sanctifying love as well. We want them to learn to give God the intelligent and loving praise for His marvelous work that only a man can give, and to give that praise as part of the great praise which our Lord is continually giving to His Father in the joy of the Holy Spirit.

Our special task as parents, here, is to lay in childhood the foundations for such an attitude, and to be always ready to show the children how to integrate into this attitude all the different kinds of information they may acquire about the make-up of the world and the universe.

For this purpose, we need first to see to it that the children actually have sufficient opportunity to see God's works: the night sky, for instance, and trees and fields and grass, and, when possible, hills and lakes, the sea and mountains. (Here is an excellent argument for at least some rural life for families!) Then, we need to equip ourselves with an elementary knowledge of the natural sciences dealing with the make-up and functioning of the universe, the solar system, our earth. We also need a good working knowledge of the nature of Psalms, in particular, 8, 18, 28, 64, 95, 96, 97, 103, 147, 148 and the Canticle of the Three Children in the fiery furnace.

Equipped with such knowledge, we may be able to lead the children from their initial wonder at, say, the sky full of stars, to a greater wonder resulting from some real knowledge of what the stars are, their distance from us and each other etc., to the praise of God as expressed in human words by the Holy Spirit Himself. And if we can make it habitual so to proceed from the observed facts of nature to the praise of God, whenever the children's interest, some new view or piece of knowledge, some startling event like a big storm, make it natural to do so, then we will be laying the true and right foundations for a life-long attitude toward all natural science.

And, as the children grow older, we can continue to deepen and broaden the scope of this habit in all its dimensions. We can encourage the children to observe accurately, to study and think about natural science of all kinds (even by making collections of odd bugs or butterflies); we can find out from bookstores or libraries where to get more detailed scientific information about whatever most interests the children; we can absorb enough of this information ourselves to give the children the habit of looking first for the *purpose* for which God made anything and made it the way it is; then to admire how marvelously the design, material and functioning of the thing is adapted to this purpose.

We can continually try to complement the children's experience and growing knowledge of nature and natural things with an ever-growing appreciation of the way in which these things are used by our Lord and in Holy Scripture as signs and "types" of His relations with us, of His life in the Church, and of our lives with Him hereafter.

For example, Christian tradition has always seen the sun as a "type," a sign of our Lord. Any child's spontaneous reaction to the wonder of a sunrise, or of a glorious sunny day after many dark ones, can be made a basis for some growth in the knowledge and love of our Lord as the Sun of our lives. And any scientific knowledge about the action of the sun on all the water of the world, for example, or in photosynthesis, can be used as material to fill out and expand the analogy, to lead the growing and grown-up mind and heart to God.

Perhaps our whole aim in all this can most powerfully and beautifully be summed up in one paragraph from St. Bonaventure's *The Journey of the Mind into God*. For we want to train our children so that they will always be free from the blindness, deafness, dumbness and stupidity he speaks of, and train them so that they may be able to awaken others to use all material creation as 'material for glory', for praising the glory of God and so achieving glory themselves:

"He must be blind, then, who is not enlightened by the great splendors of created things; he must be deaf who is not awakened by such loud outcries; he must be dumb who does not praise God for all these effects of His power; he must be stupid who is not led to the First Principle by all these indications in His work.

61

"Open your eyes, then; listen attentively with the ears of your spirit; move your lips and direct your heart, so that in all created things you may see, hear, praise, love, serve, magnify and honor your God; if you do not, the whole world may rise together against you.

"For it is for this reason that *the whole world will fight against the unwise*. But for those who are wise, the world will rather become material for glory, for those who can say with the Prophet: *'Thou hast delighted me, Lord, with Thy making, and I will exult in the work of Thy hands. How wonderful are Thy works, O Lord, Thou hast made everything in wisdom, the earth is filled with Thy possessions.'*"

But we need to show our children also how the great works of man's hands are meant to lead our minds and hearts to God. A Christian is crippled for God's service if he cannot see what is good and wonderful in a great city, a great bridge or dam, a great building; if such things do not give him material for thinking of and loving and praising God, as well as reasons for shrinking from evil.

Of course, we need not try to blind ourselves or the children to the evils involved in the very existence of a big modern city, of a skyscraper, of a great factory. But the thrill that comes to anyone at the sight of the New York skyline, or the Golden Gate Bridge[1] can just as well be ordered to God as that which comes, say, from the Grand Canyon; and if it is not, a whole side of our children's lives will be allowed to grow up cut off from God and His love.

So we need to direct the children's admiration for man's

[1] It is our own experience of such a thrill, for instance, which makes us able to appreciate the wonder of the pilgrims at the glorious sight of Jerusalem: "Thou city built into one perfect whole!" (Psalm 121), and so to appreciate what our spiritual emotions should be at the vision of the Church on earth and in heaven.

wonderful works to an admiration for God who made men able to discover how to make these things, able to get together and actually build them. Again, when opportunity permits, from the sight of all the ordered activity that goes on in putting up a new building, for example, we can show the children how we should all be working to build up God's house; from the care with which each brick or rivet is put in its right place, we can lead them to think about the care with which God is fashioning us with "blows and strokes" as the stones of His eternal dwelling.

When they come to experience the life of a great city, or to learn about city organization and so on, we can show them that it is by no mistake of terminology that the Church is called the "City" of God; that the company of redeemed mankind will be the holy city, the new Jerusalem coming down from God; and, therefore, it is part of the Christian's work to make our human cities less completely unlike the heavenly one, to see to it that life in these cities is better suited to lead men toward that heavenly City rather than away from it into that of the devil.

Along these lines also, we can begin to give the children some sense of the Church at work all over the world, leavening with Christ's own presence and action cities and towns, villages and country, wherever there is a priest at work, wherever there are Christians building up the kingdom of God. And so we can begin to give the children a world-wide vision of the Church at work, of its needs in various countries, of our responsibility to pray for and support all missionary effort.

Such a vision will mean also what might be called a Catholic sense of geography, which sees Rome as the real nerve-center of the world, the home of Christ's Vicar and of all the organizations by means of which he governs the world-wide Church. Such a Catholic sense of geography is also aware of the great spiritual centers in each country, of the great shrines of our faith, of the Holy Land as what it is.

But above all it sees the world as being vivified and renewed by the invisible force of Christ's life working through the visible organization of the Church, reaching from the Holy Father in Rome to our Bishop in his Cathedral, to our own parish Church in which we receive the teaching, the life and the direction of Christ Himself.

It is hard for a 'born' Catholic to realize how featureless must be the lives of those whose ordinary experience does not include any kind of a 'holy place.' All other cultures have had places known to be especially filled with the power of their god or gods or demons; only to ours is everywhere equally neutral, equally empty of any presence above or below or beyond the human. But since we live in such a culture, we need to do something to cultivate in ourselves and our children a real and living sense of the sacredness of our churches. "This is a place to fill one with awe," says the Introit of the Feast of the Dedication of our own church, "Truly it is the House of God and the gate of heaven."

One seldom-used means of giving our children such a sense of our church's holiness might be to ask our pastor or his assistant to give a private (or, better, public) description of the marvelous ceremony of consecration (if ours is a consecrated church, or of its blessing, if it is not). Surely such a description would make a wonderful sermon for the anniversary of consecration or blessing.

Again, we might ask our pastor to take the children, as a priest friend of ours actually does, on a conducted tour of the church, showing them the consecration crosses, letting them have a good look at the altar and its furnishings, at the holy oils in the ambry, at the sacred vessels and vestments for Mass, while he tells them as much as they could follow of the special blessings of each thing and of its use.

Besides such special means, we must, of course, take the day by day ordinary means of teaching the children to appreciate the holiness of our church by teaching them to appreciate the wonders that take place in it: the Mass, especially the Sunday Mass, Baptisms, Confirmation, Confessions, blessings, prayers made and heard, the Presence of our Lord in the Blessed Sacrament.

We also need to give the children a sense of the sacredness of places in which Christians live and work, not that this is of the same kind or degree as the sacredness of a church, but it is nonetheless very real in its own right. The most obvious among such places is, of course, our own home. We need to bring the children to feel implicitly that their home is, as it were, their special workshop, training-ground, gymnasium in the work and exercises of real life, and not to feel that real living takes place everywhere else, that home is simply a filling-station for their physical or spiritual needs. (Though, of course, they will always feel at times that other people's homes are more interesting, more full of promise and vitality than their own.)

And, by the time they grow up, they should realize that it is now their task to go out and form some new home, whether in a rectory, or a convent, or a group, or a new 'little church,' an ordinary Catholic home. But for the years of their home-life we should surely try to make them feel positively and not merely negatively "at home at home." And for this purpose, we need to make sure that real living, spiritual and mental, as well as physical, is going on in our house. If we ourselves are trying to lead a fully Christian home life, surely this effect will follow.

In this regard, we can also try to make sure that the physical lay-out, furnishing, decoration, etc., of our houses are, as far as possible, suited to the life we are trying to lead in them, not to somebody else's life, or to some notion of static unrumpled perfection.

So we can try to train the children in habits of order and tidiness; teach them to help us with the cleaning and beautifying of the house by showing them that all this is for the sake of more efficient, more fruitful, more vital living both human and Christian; that if your tools for carpentry, or for cooking, or for clothing yourself are so mixed up that you cannot find what you want, such a mess is neither practical nor efficient, nor worthy of a house in which Christ's members and fellow-workers live and work.

So, also, we can not only have our houses blessed when we first move in and, when possible, at Epiphany and Eastertime, but we can try to make these blessings really understood by the children as vital forces in our home life, forces with which we want to cooperate in order to live as fully and happily as God intends.

In this connection also, we can try to give the children the sense of going away from home and coming back as special events. For instance, one mother known to the writer is careful always to give her children a blessing, the sign of the Cross on their foreheads, before they go out, even to school or to a friend's house to play.

We can also work towards awakening in the children a sense of responsibility about going to other people's houses, being sure they are invited generally or specifically, telling us just where they are going, and being back home again on time. And, above all, we can try to make sure, in our discussions of our home furnishings and improvements, and in our comments on other people's houses, that our children come to understand that it is not the material or size or plan or efficiency or "niceness" or "loveliness" of beautiful surroundings or furnishings that are important about a house, but rather the Christian life of charity that is lived in it—that all these other things are only important as possible means toward this end.

As the children grow older, of course, they will realize more and more explicitly that, although God is everywhere, there are many places, alas, in which He is not wanted, to which He is never invited, and many from which He is as positively excluded as the perversity of human (and devilish) wills can do it. Our task here, it would seem, is to be aware of children's instinctive reaction to the presence of evil in places, to encourage them to realize that our Lord has, in fact, overcome all this, and that they can overcome it also in His strength with the sign of His Cross.

We can show them also that their future work as Christians is to be our Lord's instruments in bringing His life and grace to the human beings who are responsible for the unholiness of unholy places, and so helping Him to restore all places as signs of His presence. And we can also reassure them, whenever the need presents itself, that in deepest truth, unless by unrepented serious sin they have cut themselves off from God's presence, wherever they go they will find, ultimately, "only God and nothing strange."

1. What is the Christian attitude toward nature?

2. List the ways in which children can be aided in acquiring an understanding of nature.

3. How can children be led to appreciate that the parish church is a place of special reverence?

4. In what ways can we give a religious meaning to our own home?

5. What standard should children use in judging the homes of other people?

ðiscussion topics

I List examples of how the Church uses some places or some aspect of nature as a symbol for religious truth. (Consult the litanies and Scripture; for example, the Blessed Virgin as "Ark of the Covenant.")

2. Discuss the importance of religious places in our lives. Do we have the same concern for learning about the sacred places in our area (such as the Cathedral church and religious institutions in our dioceses) as we have for places of civic interest? Would it be possible to arrange pilgrimages to various religious places in the area?

3. A conscientious Christian housewife said: "One of the things that bothers me is that now with several children I can't keep the house as tidy as I would like to have it." Discuss this problem and try to set a standard to guide a Christian mother in her housekeeping: can there be too much "order"? too little order?

4. Discuss ways of building an appreciation for Rome and the various European countries through which we have received our Christian culture.

5. Discuss the places in the community where "God is positively excluded." Do teenagers have difficulty in recognizing the places where God is excluded and the places that are occasions of sin? What kind of program can be suggested which would encourage teenage recreation at places and in ways consistent with Christian culture?

6 WORK

"What are you going to do when you finish school?"
"Oh, get some kind of a job, I guess."

How many Catholic young men and women today give this vague and dreary answer to a question which should call forth intelligence and heroism, zeal and hope! And how many of us who are now parents, even those of us who had good Catholic parents and a good Catholic education, look back regretfully on many dismal years spent in finding out what our lives were for, convinced as we were that since God had not given us a priestly or religious vocation, He had no special plans for us at all.

But it is part of our faith itself to believe that God has a special plan, a vocation, for everyone, and that means for each of our children. And it is part of our faith to believe that this plan of His for each child is an integral part of His plan for the whole human race, for the upbuilding of the whole mystical Body of Christ to its final perfection.

Surely, then, one of our main tasks as parents must be to

give our children a positive and realistic idea of the Christian vocation as a whole, and of the various vocations, professions, and occupations by which that vocation may be carried out by Christ's members. And we must also do everything in our power to equip our children to find out and to fulfill the part which God has given each of them in His great plan.

Obviously, all our home life, all our education and training should tend to give our children the great plan of the Christian vocation, "to know Him and the power of His resurrection and the fellowship of His sufferings . . . doing the truth in charity, to grow up in all things in Him who is the Head."

But even if we teach our children the outlines of this great plan, even if we also show it to them in our daily living, our education may yet fail of its purpose if we do not give them some idea of the various ways in which this great plan actually is to be furthered by daily Christian life and work, of how it may be furthered not only by a man's general 'state in life,' but by the works of that state and, in particular, by the work by which he earns his daily bread.

For unless God gives our children a clear and early vocation to the priesthood or religious life, the necessities of earning a living will face them as soon as their schooling is over. And if we have not managed to show them how 'real life' and earning a living, in all its rightful forms, is meant to be part of the Christian vocation, the vision we have tried to give them of God's plan may well prove to be more of a torment than a guide, more a cause of schizophrenia than of sanctity. And what a waste!

Let us begin, then, to give ourselves as clear an idea as possible of all the rightful forms of human work, of how each of these has been 'Christ-ened' by our Lord's own example and by the grace He gives us to work in Him and for Him, and of how each is meant, in God's plan to contribute to the building up of Christ's Body and to the reestablishment of all things in Christ. For if we ourselves can truly see how the work of a farmer, a storekeeper, a train-dispatcher, as well as that of a doctor or teacher or priest can be truly a share in Christ's work, then we will be prepared to give our children an intelligent and comprehensive idea of real life and of the possibilities of their own future lives.[1]

Moreover, if our children really possess the Christian idea of work, then they will be able, with God's grace, to help make sense out of life for their fellows in high school or college, in their neighborhood or place of work, at that most trying and difficult age when one wants the best, but is learning to expect the worst. What a marvelous opportunity for charity this would be, were more Catholic young people trained to take advantage of it!

If we consider human nature, then, in the light of Christian teaching, we see that God made men as incomplete creatures, needing each other's services and many kinds of material and spiritual goods and services in order to exist and grow and perfect themselves. We see also that God made men to His image and likeness so that they could fulfill each other's needs and their own. As God is our Creator, He made men able to be makers: as He is Truth itself, He made men able to be teachers, communicating what they learn of His wisdom to each other. And as He is Goodness and Love, the end of all human wills, He made men able to rule and guide one another toward the ends of human life.

The work of mankind, then, consists in one way or another in making, teaching, and ruling, and, because of the

[1] See *My Book About God* by Julie Bedier (MacMillan) for a wonderful presentation for children of different kinds of work as God sees them.

very relation of men to God, in the work of uniting men to God, the work of priesthood. Farmers, herdsmen, miners, builders, storekeepers, businessmen, all who work to make or produce or make available goods and services, are, obviously, makers, and many of them are also rulers of their enterprises and of those who work under them.

A doctor is a maker of health and a teacher, as his name implies, of how to become healthy. A lawyer is (or should be) a maker of peace and order and a teacher of how to achieve it. A writer is a teacher of some aspect of wisdom and a maker of the story or play or poem or article by which he communicates his vision to others.

Now all this four-fold work of mankind was planned by God in the beginning. But it has been, obviously, warped and thwarted and perverted in many ways by sin and sinfulness throughout human history, as it has been made arduous and difficult in punishment for original sin. But it has all now been redeemed and consecrated by Christ our Lord, so that men can now, in Him and through Him, work as befits God's children.

Our Lord was anointed with the Oil of Gladness of the Holy Spirit at the very beginning of His human life, to be the Priest, the King and the Prophet of all mankind (see the Preface for the Feast of Christ the King and the ceremony for the Consecration of Holy Chrism). And the great work which His Father gave Him to do of making us all into a Kingdom, included during His life on earth the ordinary human work of making tools and furniture at Nazareth, and of making stories and sermons in His public life.

Since, then, by Baptism and Confirmation, we share in our Lord's life and His powers, His work and His purpose, we can in very truth work in Him, with Him and for Him. We can make the work by which we earn our daily bread

a part of our Lord's one great work of building up the Kingdom of God.

In the first place, as we all realize from the words of the
Morning Offering, because of our share in Christ's Priesthood
as baptized and confirmed Christians, we can offer our lives
and work and sufferings to God with Christ's sacrifice in the
Mass. We were incorporated into Christ's mystical Body by
Baptism. Our vitality as members of that Body is increased as
we grow in grace; we are living and useful members to the
degree of our union with Christ in love.

According to the degree of this union, according to the
measure in which our life is at the service of Christ's life,
our activity is somehow united with His so as to share in
the value of His great work. The more perfectly Christian
we are, then, the more whatever we do and suffer is united
with His work and suffering, represented in the Mass, for
the redemption of mankind. In this way, all our work and
suffering, whatever its other value, may be transformed into
a positive contribution towards the greater vitality, growth
and perfection of the whole mystical Body, the welfare of
mankind and the glory of God.

One of the deepest and most glorious truths of our faith
certainly is that what is only waste and loss in terms of
temporal value—mistakes, suffering, failure, and death itself
—can, in Christ, have the greatest possible value, individual
and social, for all eternity.

But our attempts to realize this should not make us forget
that ordinary human work which does produce temporal
results can also have, in Christ, its eternal value. No normal
man wants to spend his time and strength and energy on
mere busy-work or boondoggling. And normal men resent,
at least subconsciously, that so-called Christian view of work
which would make of it only a punishment, or a kind of

busy-work to keep us out of trouble during our earthly exile.[1]

But this is, of course, nowhere near the glorious Christian truth. The fact is that all rightful human work duly satisfies a real God-given or God-permitted human need, has the eternal value of helping to build up the kingdom of God, the Body of Christ, to its full and everlasting perfection.[2] The City of God is "not made with hands," the houses and statues we make will not last for eternity, neither will the books we write, the laws we frame, the institutions we establish. But the effects of all these things on the human beings who are to be the living stones of God's eternal temple will last forever.

The way in which a man is fed, clothed and housed, the way in which he is taught, ruled, and entertained, given the tools and conditions under which he himself does his work— all this affects the quality of his human living (and so of the meritorious value of his actions); all this aids or hampers his achieving his final perfection as the unique member of Christ's Body that God means him to be for all eternity.

When our Lord said: "Whatever you do to these My least brethren, you do to Me," He meant it as a fact, not as a mere manner of speaking, for in feeding, clothing, comforting, advising, guiding one another, we are actually 'edifying,' that is, building up the members of Christ's own Body.

[1] If one may say so in all reverence, the common notion of the value of making the Morning Offering is that it turns our work into a kind of heavenly boondoggling (work which, people think, has no eternal value in itself; whether it be well or badly done, if we 'offer' it to God, He will pay us eternal wages for it in consideration of the merits of Christ).

[2] Here is the truth about work which, largely forgotten by Christians, has been re-discovered by Communism, and warped and perverted to make only the perfection of the City of Man its end and justification.

Only God himself knows, of course, when and to what extent His grace makes up for our mistakes and failures and mistreatment in fulfilling each other's needs, so that somehow, in spite of all this, 'all manner of things shall be well' and the perfection of the mystical Body and each of its members finally and beautifully achieved. But we do know that we shall be judged and given our place for all eternity on how we have tried to fulfill each other's needs . . . "Come," or "Go" as we fed, clothed, housed, comforted Him in His brethren.[1]

We can easily see that a well-planned and well-built house, for instance, contributes to the possibility of men's living a good and Christian life. The lack of proper housing is one of the chief occasions of sin and discouragement today; a poorly planned and built house is a source of irritation, of waste of thought and energy that might have been put into prayer or study or needed relaxation or the fruitful service of others.

But a house planned for the needs of those who live in it and built as well as a house can be, conduces to contentment, to hospitality, to good human living and so to the more effective service of God and our neighbor. Clearly, then, the work of the architect, of the contractor, of all the craftsmen who gave their time and strength and skill to building such a house, in actual fact contributes objectively

[1] To make this truth real and vital to ourselves, study-clubs, sodalities, etc., could follow the example of a group in Louisiana who have made a study of how each man's work in fact aids his fellow-members of the mystical Body; the men concerned with oil, for instance, help everyone all over the country who uses the oil in furnaces, cars, etc. Those concerned with natural gas help families they will only meet in heaven to cook and heat their houses. So a man cannot always have the obvious advantages of direct person-to-person service in his work, but he can take such means as this to make its quality of loving service of Christ in others a vivid reality both to himself and to his children.

to the building up of the kingdom of God. So too, for all other forms of work.

But if our work is to have such an everlasting value (as well as a real temporal value), it must satisfy *duly* a true human need. This means that it must be done both charitably and skillfully, so that we try to find out and satisfy our neighbor's real needs rather than to seek our own gain, and that we try to satisfy these needs as well as possible, rather than try to get away with whatever a patron or customer will take. For, obviously, if the work we do is actually for the purpose of pandering to our neighbor's vices, of hindering him from leading a good life, it is serving not Christ, but the devil. And as we would certainly not offer careless, shoddy work to Christ Himself, so neither should we offer less than the best we can, or could learn to do, to Christ in our neighbor.

If we look at the list of the corporal and spiritual works of mercy, we see that it adds up to a summary catalogue of human needs in an acute form. The only difference, then, for a Christian between performing a work of mercy and doing the work by which he earns his daily bread should be that he expects no return from the work of mercy, while he expects, in justice, to receive from his daily work either enough of its products, or a fee, salary, or wage sufficient to enable him to continue to satisfy his neighbor's need by means of his own particular skill, and to support his family and bring up his children to take their due part in the work of mankind, the work of Christ.

How fruitful and how wonderful, therefore, every rightful form of human work might be! As things are, few people besides priests and religious realize that they are co-workers with Christ and that their daily work has an eternal value of its own. And so the vast majority of Christians have lost the joy of this realization, and, what is worse, have lost the norms of what constitutes true and fruitful work.

Here is one of the chief causes for the desperate state of things in the world today. For the Christian truth is only the fulfillment and perfection of the true human idea of what work should be, and today we have almost completely lost both. While, thank God, many a doctor, many a small-town storekeeper or banker, many a farmer and craftsman still works primarily for other people's welfare, yet in general all kinds of vicious and artificial wants are mistaken for true "needs," the efficiency of machines and not the true welfare of the worker or the customer is the norm for what should be made, keeping up with or getting ahead of other people are the norms for success, rather than the true service of others.

Now, surely, it is the full Christian truth about work that we must be ready to give to our children. For if they are called to any form of lay life, they will have the double vocation of carrying out their own daily work as Christians, and of doing whatever they can to re-establish their chosen profession or occupation "in Christ"; to make it easier for others to work as Christians and to produce the full effects of Christian work and so leaven the whole of society. Or, if God calls our children to be His priests or religious, a part of their vocation will be to teach and lead and guide others by work and prayer toward the Christian idea of work.

In the next chapter, then, we will consider some concrete suggestions as to how we may best communicate to our children this Christian view of work and train them to work in accordance with it.

∂ i s c u s s i o n topics

1. Discuss the place of work in the life of a Christian. Is work to be considered primarily as a punishment imposed on man? A man has an independent income sufficient to satisfy his normal needs; would this man be a better and happier person if he did not work at all?

2. Contrast the basic Christian motives for work with the prevailing secular ideas about work. Analyze the various professions in terms of how their members seem to be motivated by Christian motives of work. How many workers get satisfaction from their work because they are filling a "true human need" of someone else? How extensive is the concept that work is to provide a service for others?

3. A husband works long hours and overtime because he wants to provide the "best" for his family. The wife works regularly away from home in order to increase family income so they can buy things of the same standard as their neighbors and friends. Do their motives reflect the Christian concept of work?

4. Discuss methods of developing a Christian idea of work in children. How far can children be expected to appreciate the deeper motivations of routine work at home? The mother of a family does most of the cooking, cleaning, and sewing rather than have her daughters help because, she says, "It's easier and faster to do it myself than to try to show them how—and besides, I can do it better." Is this the Christian approach?

5. To what extent should the father share in the work of homemaking? Should the wife assume that her husband will take over the chief responsibility for family work after he gets home in the evening? Should the husband and wife share equally the necessary work on Saturday afternoons and Sunday? How does a Christian philosophy of work provide a basis for solving this problem?

1. Classify the four ways in which man works.

2. Explain the meaning of the word "works" in the Morning Offering.

3. What is the principal purpose of work?

4. Why are the conditions under which men work important?

5. What is the difference between one's regular daily work and a spiritual or corporal work of mercy?

7 training for life's work and play

In the preceding chapter, we considered the Christian idea of work. We saw how this idea means, practically, that we can each in our own degree and way, work *with* Christ in His four-fold work of making, ruling, teaching and uniting men to God; that we can work *for* Christ by serving Him in serving one another's needs; and by this service, if it is true service, on however humble a level, we can help to build up His kingdom, both by the merit of our charity and by the objective effects of our work itself. How can we, then, best communicate this idea of work to our children and how can we best train them for it?

The first means must surely be to try to give them an ever-increasing appreciation of the sacrament of Confirmation. When the children are still quite young, we could, perhaps, ask our pastor to show us the actual Holy Oils as they are treasured in our parish church, and to explain the use of each. The children have already been anointed with the Oil of Catechumens and with Holy Chrism at Baptism;

and we could tell even those who are small something of the meaning of these anointings; of why oil is used, of why a fragrant perfume is added to the oil to make Chrism, and so on. The children have already experienced many of the various uses of oil in daily life; it should not be too hard to give them the basic idea of sacramental anointings.

Then we could take the opportunity of the blessing of the Holy Oils each Holy Thursday to go over with the children the glorious prayers of the Consecration of Chrism (and of the other Oils as well), and, when it is practical, we could attend the Bishop's Mass in our Cathedral.

Again, we can do whatever is needful to supplement the instruction each child is given for the reception of the sacrament itself. We can emphasize the spiritual dignity and responsibility and maturity which Confirmation implies. And we can also emphasize its dynamic quality, that it gives them the right and makes them able to do special things for Christ.

In particular we can begin to show them that this glorious sacrament "penetrates them through and through with Christ's kingly, priestly, and prophetic honor . . . clothes them with the robes of special office" (Consecration of Holy Chrism) so that they can share in Our Lord's work of ruling and teaching and of the lay priesthood.

We can here begin to show them the connections between their daily jobs, their small responsibilities to each other, their participation in the Mass, with the effects of this sacrament. We can also go over the text of the administration of the sacrament of Confirmation and show them how these Gifts of the Holy Spirit which they are to receive are the special equipment that they need for living and working as grown-up Christians, in, with, and for Christ.

And each anniversary of a child's Confirmation can also be used to deepen the lessons of the great day itself, to integrate these lessons with all the new experiences and responsibilities of the past year. In particular we can try to connect the sacrament practically in their minds with their daily work, with their lessons, with all their training for the future, and, as they grow older, with their ideas of what their life's work might be.

Is young John, for example, age 14, trying to cooperate with the gift, let us say, of counsel? When he doesn't know what to do in a given situation, does he raise his mind and heart, does he think of asking the Holy Spirit? Does he then take all the prudent human means of consulting parents or older friends about how to face a similar situation in the future, and then ask the Holy Spirit to give him a greater share in the gift of counsel for the next occasion? Is he studying his religion lessons so as to cooperate as fully as possible with the Holy Spirit and His gifts of wisdom, understanding and knowledge, so that later on the Spirit of Love will be able to use him to tell other people about the wonderful works of God?

Perhaps the anniversary of each child's Confirmation could be used in such a way for a kind of personal check-up on the use of the graces of this sacrament, while during the novena for the great feast of Pentecost and the feast itself, the whole family could cultivate an appreciation of the sacrament of Confirmation and of its wonderful practical effects in our lives.

But, of course, none of this will be of much value to our children if we ourselves are not trying to show the effects of Confirmation in our own daily living and working, if we mothers and fathers are not trying to work *with* and *for* Christ in whatever we do, as we share in His priestly, kingly, and prophetic honor.

As far as we mothers are concerned, it is not very hard

for us to see how we ought to go about the day's work; the difficulty lies in trying actually to do it that way. For in our lives with our family, in our housework, in whatever we do over and above for our parish and our community, we women are usually concerned with meeting basic human needs, providing basic human services for people whom we personally know and love.

We can easily see, then, how our day's work consists of the whole four-fold work of mankind, the four-fold work of Christ. We share in His work of making by means of all our housework; we share in His work as Prophet as we answer the children's endless questions, in His work as Ruler when we discipline and train them. We can easily see how we are working *for* Christ in His members, in our husband, children, and neighbors. And we can see also how we are working to build up His kingdom by assisting our husbands in their life-work and by helping to build up and educate His future co-workers, our children.

Our difficulty is, of course, actually to carry out our work every day in the spirit and manner which this all implies. But, surely, some effort to think about the real significance of all the jobs we are doing, and much prayer to our Lady and St. Joseph, will help us to give that example of a Christian at work which our children should be finding in us.

As the children grow older, while we give them explicitly the ideal of Christian work, we can, perhaps, correct the inevitable defects of our example by giving them also some understanding of our own special difficulties—physical weakness, previous lack of training, etc.—as well as of our weakness and sinfulness, which have prevented us from fully realizing the ideal.

The father's part of this task of giving an example of Christian work is far more difficult than the mother's, yet it is, in many ways, even more important. For if the bread-winner of the family is doing his best with the help of God to win the bread in a Christian way, then the children will easily realize that integral Christian living in the real world is possible; that the effort to re-establish all things in Christ is a realistic program for every Christian; that man's chief channel for that effort can be and should be his own daily job. But if the father is not even considering his own work in such a light, it must be very difficult for the mother to feel that in being his "helpmate" she is helping Christ, and it would be doubly difficult to show the children how a real man can be Christ's co-worker within the frame of ordinary work and life.

One aspect of a father's task, then, would seem to be the work of examining his own job or profession in the light of Christian principles of work, to consider seriously how he personally might carry out his work in a more fully Christian way; and, how he might, on however small a scale, begin to work to bring about the changes in the whole set-up or profession which would make it more possible or more easy for everyone concerned in it to work in a more fully Christian way.

One of the best ways of undertaking this task would be, surely, wherever it is possible, to gather together any like-minded men in one's neighborhood to discuss together the problems of each man's job or profession in the light of the principles of Christian work.[1]

[1] It is ultimately, of course, the task of professional associations and of experts in each field to get together with moral theologians, determine the Christian norms for each occupation and profession, and decide on general lines of procedure best adapted to begin the transformation of what is into what should and could be. And, as yet, our Catholic professional schools and professional associations have only here and there begun to go about this task. But unless everyone who is aware of the necessity for restoring all kinds of work in Christ, according to the directives of the Popes, begins to look at his

Another and most important means of communicating the Christian idea of work to our children is by our own habits and methods of purchasing goods and services. It is, of course, impossible to be perfectly consistent as a Christian purchaser in today's world. But we can at least try, with the money and time and energy at our disposal, to patronize preferably those workmen on every level who are on the way toward Christian norms, rather than those who are working against these norms. Already, for example, most of us are aware of our duty not to patronize industries and stores which allow bad working conditions, wages, and so on, if we know about it; and we could make it our business to find out more about such matters.

We could also begin to consider the fact, admitted by anyone with much experience in the retail field, that almost every "bargain" means that somebody is getting cheated out of a just wage or price; or that one customer is paying for another customer's advantage; or that the purchaser is simply not getting a bargain at all, even though it is labelled as one. We can begin to take a good look at the "I'll get it for you wholesale" or the "I'll give you a good discount on that" type of salesmanship, and see what they imply all down the line from first producer to final consumer.[2]

We could, perhaps, spend at least the same amount of time as we now spend in hunting bargains in trying to find

own work and kind of work in the light of Christian principles, to discuss it with others, to judge what could and should be done and to begin to do it, the experts will never go to work on the real problems and no action would result from their conclusions if they did.

[2] In this connection, priests and religious might consider the effects of the "clergy discount" especially on the price of Catholic books. Since they are the most numerous purchasers of such books, this discount means in effect that the lay reader must pay extra. Is this practice, then, calculated to increase the spread of Catholic books among the laity? Or to help the Catholic book-stores who are trying to make these books available?

out where we can buy good things, produced by people who are really trying to do good work and serve their neighbor's needs. We could try to patronize the stores that, so far as we can tell, really try to give real service rather than talk about it; and to avoid those which clearly pander to vice by selling obscene magazines and comics, etc., and also those whose avowed policy is to drive all competitors out of the neighborhood or field in order to make more profits for themselves. And we could try to apply such a policy all up and down the line of the goods and services we need: in choosing our doctor, our lawyer, our banker, our investments (if any!) and so on.

Such a buying policy might seem to involve an impossible drain on the ordinary family's budget. But, as a matter of fact and in most cases, it would actually work out to the economic benefit of a family, since, for one thing, consistent purchasing at stores whose chief aim is to make profits for their owners, results in the customer's getting less than his money's worth over the years.

The family purchasing policy recommended here is certainly more in accord with the Christian idea of work (let alone of justice and charity) than is the policy of getting things as cheaply as possible for the benefit of one's own family (or community for that matter) at the expense of other families and other people. To try to buy in a Christian way is also in accord with the Christian idea of poverty, for it will mean that we have fewer and better things than if we always buy what is cheapest and easiest to get.[3]

[3] Such a policy does not mean, of course, that we are ordinarily under any obligation to patronize a workman on any level who, however good his motives, simply does not or cannot produce good work. It is no part of re-establishing all things in Christ to foster the already too prevalent Catholic vice of technical and artistic carelessness, the vice that follows on the idea that it doesn't matter what you do or how you do it so long as you "mean

We need, then, to try to give our children the Christian idea of work, especially in connection with the sacrament of Confirmation (and, obviously, with taking part in the Mass); we need also to give them this idea by means of our own example, both as workers and as patrons of other people's work. And besides, we need to make sure that the children's education includes basic training in all the four types of work, and in the Christian way of carrying them out as skillfully as possible for the love of Christ in our neighbor.

Every whole life, every vocation, every profession and most jobs require some skill in all four kinds of work, with the emphasis on one or two. Everyone needs to know how to make and to do a number of things, as well as how to share natural and supernatural truth with others, and how to exercise authority. And every Christian needs to know the basic skills of his lay priesthood, in particular how to take full and active part in the Mass (including what comes after the *Ite Missa est*), how to pray with the Church, how to continue all his life to grow in Christ by taking part in the liturgy.

We owe it to our children, then, to make sure that they get basic training in making and doing, in communicating and having something to communicate, in exercising authority, and in acting as members of the royal priesthood of the Church. For if we do not, our children will be less able to choose their life-work rightly, not knowing their own chief abilities; and they will be crippled in carrying out their life-work since they will not enter on it as well-rounded, complete co-workers with Christ.

How handicapped is the mother or father, for example,

well" and "offer it up." However "apostolic" a work may be, the apostle is obviously under the obligation as a Christian to strive for perfection in his daily work as well as in his life.

who never learned before marriage the fundamental skills involved in housekeeping and house-keeping-up, or who has never learned how to exercise any kind of authority until required to do so by the inescapable necessity of managing small children!

What, then, will this four-fold training involve in the pattern of daily family life? First of all, that we do not leave the children's religious education entirely to "Sister," but make sure ourselves, as she cannot, that our children are really learning to take part in the Mass, to pray both formally and informally, to understand God's truth in such a living fashion that they can begin to communicate it to others.

Again, we can plan how to give each of the children some chance to "run" things, to exercise authority over others, in carrying out household jobs or family projects, so that we can help them to learn what authority should mean—the good of the job and of one's fellow workers—and give them some real training and practice in exercising it during all their formative years.

We need also to plan how best to give the children some basic training in all the major forms of human communication: speaking, writing, the fine arts, dancing; as well as in gathering the knowledge and wisdom necessary in order to have something worth communicating to one's neighbor.

And we need to see that they gain the basic skills in making and doing required for ordinary human living, cooking, cleaning, washing, mending, repairing, care of animals, etc. We need also to make the effort to see that the children do whatever they are doing as thoroughly and as well as is possible under the circumstances; and that they do and learn to do things thoroughly and well, as far as possible, for the sake of Christ and for the sake of other people rather than simply for self-satisfaction or self-improvement.

At first sight, this may well seem like an impossible program for any parents even to begin to carry out. But when we begin to consider what it would involve in actual practice, we see that in trying to make sure that the children are being thus fully prepared for Christian life and work, we shall be at least on the way toward solving various other major problems of family life, perhaps the very problems which make such a complex program at first seem out of the question.

For one thing, the more we succeed in training the children to exercise due authority and to assume due responsibility in family life, the less squabbling will there be, and the less will we have to bear the whole weight of responsibility. Again, the more we succeed in teaching the children how to do household tasks reasonably well, the less will our own energy be overtasked by having to do everything ourselves. And, in so far as we can ourselves teach our children the basic skills involved in human making and communication, we will be solving also the problems of family recreation and of training the children in habits of Christian play.

The habit of reading that fosters a knowledge and love of truth, real imagination, the knowledge and skillful use of words, for example, or drawing, painting, making pottery or "sculping," singing, dancing, making up stories and plays, acting, carpentry work, gardening, etc., — all of these skills are tools both for working and playing, depending on what they are done for and how they are done. Of course, we cannot ourselves teach our children how to do all these things well, but we can at least let them try to work with us, not only in sweeping and dusting and tidying, but in making essential repairs, trying to grow our own vegetables, or whatever naturally interesting family project may be under way.

And we can also do something to give the children whatever slight skill we may be able to recover from our own childhood, if we have no more, in singing and painting and so on, so that they may at the same time learn the basic skills of artistic communication, the basic skills of grown-up play, and, actually be playing with us (as well as learning how to play without us).

One difficulty here is, of course, that most of us have to contend with our own long-established bad habits of seeking distraction in some more or less passive form of entertainment rather than in true recreation. Work and play are the same for the Wisdom of God: "I was with Him forming all things, playing before Him at all times." But for us human beings, work is basically differentiated from play by the fact that in working we have a motive beyond the activity itself (to serve our own or others' needs, to build up the kingdom of God, to do a good job, to earn a living) while in playing we have no other explicit, conscious motive than that of doing for fun what we are doing. And for us, fallen children of Adam, work also involves drudgery (conscious effort sustained far beyond the point of interest or delight) whereas play does not.

Play or recreation, however, should not be primarily passive, any more than should work. We are made in the image of God who is pure Act. We are made primarily to act; rest is only necessary because of the weakness of our physical nature. Recreation and play should, therefore, delightfully exercise our powers, especially those which are mainly unused by our day's work.[1]

[1] Here, of course, is the value of games, both for children and adults. Our responsibility here is to see that our children learn to play, rather than to look on, learn to handle themselves adequately in the legitimate games and sports common to their age and neighborhood, and how to choose their games wisely to suit their own needs and circumstances.

It would seem, then, that the more passive the form of entertainment or recreation, the less it has any legitimate place in normal living. The proper role of most "good" or "harmless" television shows, radio programs, detective stories, movies, etc., is that of soothing, amusing and entertaining invalids or shut-ins or very elderly people, or those who are so completely exhausted by inhuman forms of work or the inhuman strains of modern life that they do not have the energy for true re-creation.

Here is another difficulty about any sort of family play: most of us parents think that we are in this last condition. But let us make sure that there is nothing that we can do to increase our energy (such as getting to bed early two or three nights a week), before we entirely give up the idea of trying to play with our children!

A more serious objection is that most of us suffer in one way or another from that American snobbishness of "I never could draw a straight line . . . I just can't sing a note . . ." which we ourselves were trained to think sufficient excuse for not being fully human, not possessing some of the basic skills of all mankind. And the greatest difficulty of all lies in the habits and ways of thought of our whole modern society, of which the children will feel the pressure more and more increasingly as they grow up.

But we can all do something, beginning with the natural talents and with the already existing interests of ourselves and the children; and we can try to make their increasingly active interests call on new and greater skills of various kinds. The ideal, of course, is to center the family's work and play and acquisition of skills on the daily and seasonal liturgy, and so grow up integrally in wisdom and age and grace. To celebrate a feast or fast by special household work, singing special songs, praying special prayers, acting out some relevant scene, etc. . . ., all this makes the most truly integrated and Christian method of family life and training.

Too many of us, certainly, simply cannot imagine ourselves or our children (especially teen-age children) being willing or able to live consistently according to such a program. But we can all start from wherever we and the children are, and from their already existing interests, and try to begin from there to make our recreation truly re-creative.

And there is another vitally important effect of proper training in work and play, an effect which is so essential to the children's future Christian lives that no effort can be too great to achieve it. This is that the children retain and continue to grow in enjoyment of doing, and of doing for others. Children are naturally participants in, not passive spectators of, worship and work and play. Many of the forces bent on the destruction of Christianity are out to destroy this natural tendency, to make passivity and enjoyment seem inseparable, to make normal activity of body or mind seem unnatural and disagreeable, so that human nature may be remoulded to the image of a machine, instead of to that of God, who is pure Act.

One of our special responsibilities as parents today is, then, to see to it that our children's natural interest in real and rightful doing receives its proper nourishment, encouragement and guidance; that we do not let it die out for lack of something to do or for lack of materials and training, or be smothered out of existence by a surfeit of passively-enjoyed pleasures.

For example, how many a small child's desire to sing has been murdered by some teacher who told him to keep quiet because he had a voice like a crow. The teacher wanted her chorus to "sound well" to the other teachers and to parents, when she should have wanted all her pupils to learn to use their voices as God intended, for His praise and their own joy.

Or, again, how many a child's normal desire to paint and draw has died an unnatural death because he "had no talent," as his teachers or parents thought, and so was given no help at the critical age when he began to care how his productions looked to himself and to other people.

How many a young gardener or cook has been thwarted by lack of his parent's interest and help, because it was easier for them to do things by themselves than to teach him to help. When their normal desire to do things is frustrated, both children and grown-ups take refuge in passivity and escapism, or in vandalism (which is a form of escapism), or worse; and the means of taking refuge are all too easy to find today.

Since this is true in worship and in work and in play, let us encourage our children by every means our ingenuity can suggest, in every sphere, to become "doers of the word and not hearers only." Nor need we fear that in so doing we shall turn our children into mere activists. On the contrary, training in true, purposeful, skillful, charitable action is the best possible preparation for true contemplation. It is training in passive inaction which leads to purposeless, nervous over-activity. How can we expect the children to delight in Him who is pure Act, unless they learn to delight in human actions that have the beauty of rightness and skill and charity?

The aim of all our home training in work and play, then, should be that the children not only know how to go about the fundamental kinds of work and the skills of human living, that they have the spiritual, emotional and physical skills needed for truly human and Christian recreation, but, above all, that they have never un-learned the lesson all children know, that real happiness is to be found in true human action, not in "being amused."

And, beyond this, we need to encourage them to find their joy not only in action, but in generous action. Some children know this instinctively; others have to learn it by more or less difficult lessons all through the years of their lives. But we can assist the work of grace by giving the children the skills to be generous with; by showing them how to use them to give pleasure to others; by making generosity seem the normal and happy quality it should be in our family life; by rewarding a child's generosity with his things or his time or his strength by our expression of gratitude, and by showing him that his generosity makes it possible for us to be more generous to him.

By all these means, then, we will be laying the foundations for that highest lesson which only God's grace can teach our children that the greatest joy of all is to be found in "spending oneself and being spent for the sake of the elect." If our children have begun to learn that lesson by the time they reach maturity, then we need have no fears about their future, for they will have the basic preparation for whatever form of Christ-like action that the Lord has in mind for them.

1. What is the connection between the sacrament of Confirmation and work?

2. How do the Gifts of the Holy Spirit, especially counsel, help us in our daily work?

3. How does the work of the housewife fill the four-fold work of Christ?

4. List the basic responsibilities of parents for their children's development, as outlined by the author.

5. Explain the difference between active and passive entertainment, and summarize the author's attitude toward passive recreation.

Discussion topics

1. Review the author's evaluation of motives and methods of purchasing goods. Is it true that bargains mean that "somebody is getting cheated" or else that the bargain label is only a label? Is there room for improvement in our methods and motives of purchasing? What might be the effects on children if they observe failures in justice and charity in their parents in the economic area?

2. List practical suggestions for activity by the children (at the various age levels) which will help them develop a Christian sense of responsibility. Is it possible to put too much responsibility on children before they are ready for it? to give them too little?

3. Discuss practical ways for enabling children to achieve active forms of work and recreation to offset the temptation to be mere viewers of TV and movies. What encouragement do we offer our children for group games? for good reading? for dancing? playing musical instruments? Would it be possible for like-minded Christian families to adopt an informal program so their children could enjoy Christian recreation together?

4. Discuss ways and means of raising standards in regard to the quality of things made and purchased. What should be done to develop an appreciation for classical music? for artistic paintings and statues and home furnishings? What can be suggested for raising the level of sacred art in the home?

5. Discuss the author's emphasis on the fact that Christian living is dominated by the idea of "enjoyment of doing, and of doing for others." What are the sources of the Christian's joy? What natural and supernatural means are available to aid the Christian family in achieving this joyous atmosphere?

8 vocations

The whole purpose of all our work as parents is, of course, to prepare our children to cooperate with God's grace, to choose the vocation He has ready for them and to carry out that vocation to the full. In the last two chapters, we have been considering this aspect of the children's preparation for life here and hereafter, how to give them some understanding of the whole fourfold work of Christians in this world, and some experience and training in each kind. It may be well, therefore, to consider next how we may best give them a realistic idea of each of the chief ways of life, or what are commonly called "vocations" in the Church.

The first essential here is, obviously, that, by the time the children reach an age to choose their own way of life, they may have some real grasp of the Christian vocation as a whole. We must try to make sure, in other words, that they realize that their lives on earth are given them for the purpose of being united with, conformed to, Christ in His

Passion and Death so as to share with Him in the glory of His Resurrection.

In terms of the life ahead of them, this realization implies that the children understand that no way of life is meant to be easy, that they have no right to future freedom from want or care. It means that they look forward to life as an heroic adventure, a chance to spend themselves and be spent with Christ for the sake of His members.

It means that they understand, as well as young people can, that many stretches of their lives will seem painful, many will seem difficult, many will seem dull, but that all this is a sharing in Christ's Cross with the assurance of sharing in His victory, and all this, if lived with Christ and for the glory of God's love, will be permeated with the vitality and joy of the Holy Spirit.

Young people are normally heroic-minded, they want to be called on for heroism, they want to be convinced that their strength and talents can be used for some great cause. We shall, therefore, have the assistance both of grace and nature in giving them the Christian view of their future lives.

On the other hand, we shall obviously have to contend with the whole tone of the society in which we and our children are living, which encourages young people to believe that security and success, especially security, are the two chief aims of life, that one is entitled to a "good living," especially if one has had a "good education," that if one obeys all the rules one will inevitably "get ahead." And we shall also have to take into account the depressing undertones registered in much modern literature and in the actual mental and emotional state of innumerable ordinary citizens, that life actually is a rather dreary fuss about very little, so you might as well get as much out of it as you can when you are young.

We shall need, then, to try to debunk both these ideas, to offset both these mental tones, as the children become aware of them and begin to react to them. We shall have to show the children from actual cases, first, that no human life is in fact easy or inevitably prosperous, and that in any case people who are called successful are not necessarily happy.

We shall have to show them that, in consequence, when our Lord gives us the chance to use our lives for Him, following Him in His Passion, He is not making our lives dismal—as if they could be comfortable and serene if we were allowed to live them on a purely natural level; rather He is taking the stuff of actual human life which is, by and large, dreary and dismal indeed when it is not lived in Him and for Him, and giving it real meaning and purpose, glorifying it with the glory of His victory over death and sin, and making it truly joyful with the joy of His resurrection.

Giving the children this dynamic pattern of Christian life, at least implicitly, is of course the supreme work of all the years of their training. But at the time when they are seriously beginning to think of their choice of a way of life, they will want and need trusted advisors other than their parents. We should, then, look forward to this time when explicit teaching from us about the future will probably be of no use to our children, and try to see to it that they have come to know and trust and confide in other people, laymen, religious, and priests, who are endeavoring to live heroically Christian lives. Our part then will probably be that of prayer; whatever else we can do to help our children find their vocation will, in the main, have been done already.

Within the unity of the one Christian pattern of life, the great Christian vocation, the children will need to know something of each of the chief ways of Christian life and of the special place of each in carrying out the one work of Christ, the redemption of mankind.[1] Of course, nobody can fully appreciate what a vocation implies until one is actually living it; but one can know what are its essential features according to God's plan, what are accidentals, and what each vocation is not meant to be.

But we owe our children at least that much of a grasp of all the great "vocations" in the Church, so that they may have all the information they need in order to cooperate intelligently and freely with God's grace in their choice of a vocation, and also that they may be better fitted to carry out that vocation fully. For, since all vocations are meant by God to contribute their own share to the one work of Christ, the more a man appreciates what other people are doing, the better can he carry out his own special task. The greater the priest, the more fully he appreciates the work of laity and religious; the greater the layman, the more he appreciates his priests and religious, and so on.

We want our children, then, to see a vocation to the priesthood as a call to become another Christ in the very special sense of taking part in His work of mediation between God and man in a unique and special way. All Christians share by Baptism and Confirmation in our Lord's office as Priest; but our share can only be made fully operative by the special work of the ordained priesthood.

We marry and have children to bring to the font of re-birth in Christ; the priest baptizes them. We train them to be Christ's soldiers and co-workers; the Bishop gives them by Confirmation their actual commission and the powers to

---

[1] What follows is not meant to be a complete theological description of each vocation, but a working or practical one in terms of characteristic functions.

act on it. We gather human learning and experience; the priest teaches us God's truth from day to day so that in its light and by its power we may continually transform our human experience into Christian wisdom.

We rule ourselves and our families and our businesses to try to provide the necessary order, the conditions of human and Christian living; the priest rules some part of Christ's flock so as to make our lives fruitful for life everlasting.

We bring to the sacrifice of the Mass our whole lives and work, along with the money our work has earned to provide the materials for the sacrifice; the priest transforms the bread and wine into the Body and Blood of Christ, makes it possible for us to offer ourselves in His offering, and gives us Christ's Body in holy Communion to unite us together in love, to give us the energy for Christian living, to transform us into Him.

It is the work of Christ's priest, then, to unite God and man, to make the life of the people of God both possible and fruitful. He it is who, as Christ's special instrument, gives other people's lives their Christian meaning and value. Like the Holy Father himself, the chief Shepherd of Christ's flock on earth, every priest is the "servant of the servants of God," and so he achieves his own sanctity by this splendid and selfless service.

Thus the priest's vocation is unique. He is part of the teaching, ruling, sanctifying hierarchy of the Church; all the rest of us make up the *laos,* the People of God, all leading the one Christian life.

Now the highest way of living this Christian life is, of course, as a religious. For religious are called to specialize in the acts of the virtue of religion, the acts that directly bind man to God: taking part in the Mass, the Divine Office, prayer. We married people ordinarily have to subordinate to the works and duties of our own state in life more than the essential minimum of such strictly "religious" actions. But for the religious they constitute, as laid out in his Rule, the very essence of his daily life.

Again, religious are called to specialize directly in living and perfecting themselves in the bridal relationship of the Church with Christ. We all share in this relationship as Christians; it is the very purpose of our existence; but married people are called to work towards perfect union with Christ as it were indirectly, by learning and practicing the love of each other in Christian marriage. Religious, on the other hand, explicitly by vow, deny themselves the symbol, and go straight toward the reality, the eternal Marriage of redeemed mankind with Christ.

In the same way, we who are in the world try to use goods and possessions rightly so as to bring them into the sphere of Christ's life and work, so as to help to restore all things in Him. But religious deny themselves the free use of possessions so as to be freer for the work of uniting themselves to God. We who are in the world are sanctified by our obedience to God's will as it is shown to us in the Commandments, in the duties of our state and work, and in all the circumstances of our lives. But religious are called to take the far clearer and surer way of obedience, under the Commandments, to their Rules and to their Superiors.

A vocation to the religious life is, then, a call to a state of life higher and more extraordinary than that of marriage and lay life in the world for the reason that it dispenses with the, so to speak, slower and more indirect means of sanctification which are necessary for the majority of Christians. The religious life takes a difficult but clear and straight short-cut to the summit of the mountain; married and lay life is planned by God to arrive at the same goal by a less clear, more winding path which has been suited by His mercy to the needs of His ordinary children.

There is also the vocation which seems to be a special answer to the special needs of today—a life of dedicated virginity in the world, lived in family-like groups, whose purpose it is to give an example of integral Christian living, and to work out ways and means of helping other people to live fully Christian lives. This vocation is essentially "lay," in that it implies no withdrawal from the world (using the word in its good sense, as in "God so loved the world"), but rather a special study and effort to carry out the lay vocation of using the things of the world rightly.

It also shares in the complete dedication of self directly to Christ, which is characteristic of the religious. The vocation to a lay institute would seem to be a call to live the life of a religious, but, because of one's special circumstances or work, to lead this life in the world, not in a cloister.

The special characteristic of a vocation for a single Christian "in the world" consists in its freedom to concentrate on carrying out some particular work for the sake of Christ and His members. A priest is bound to answer the call of his bishop in serving the flock of Christ as a priest. No special taste, talent or training for, say, writing or teaching chemistry or scientific research can be put ahead of his obedient service as a priest of Christ's flock.

The religious is also bound primarily by his whole rule of life, by the day's schedule and by his obedient service of the good of the whole community. His superiors may take his special tastes, talents, or training into consideration in assigning him to his work, or they may not; he may be changed from one field to another overnight, if the good of his soul and the community demands it.

Obviously, too, married people are obligated first of all to the duties and demands of their state of life. Husband and wife are bound, ordinarily to arrange their lives so as to have time and energy to perfect their married life; parents are bound, again in general, to keep sufficient time and energy for the work of parenthood. Only the single Christian "in the world" is free to concentrate on his work, to put his special work for God and his neighbor above the demands of a whole pattern of life directed toward the same service.

This characteristic of freedom *from* the demands of a special Christian pattern of life *for* a particular form of Christian work gives this state of life its value as a preparation for the other vocations of Christian living. It leaves young men and women free to try various kinds of work, free to prepare themselves for some special work and to get started in it, before they take on a whole pattern of life into which that work must be fitted.

Since our children will certainly be leading this single life "in the world" from the time that they take over the responsibility for arranging their own lives until they enter, if they do, into the priesthood or religious life or marriage (all during the years of their college and professional training, for instance), we should give them some idea of its special value and of its special hazards, the hazards that arise out of its very freedom from a pattern or from the demands of the other ways of life.

Various kinds of formal dedication to the single Christian life and to some special work are ways of making explicit the fact that this way of life is not meant to be only a stage on the road to other vocations, but may also be a true vocation in itself. And this vocation lacks the safeguards, the supports, the frame-work of the others, while it puts itself at the service of all the others. Christian family living, the works of the priesthood and religious, all are made less difficult and more fruitful by the work of the single Christian. All of us should in gratitude give him or her the honor that is due to one who is pursuing such a great vocation of service, whether it was more or less inspired by the will of God under the guise of circumstances, or undertaken of set purpose.

As our children begin to ask questions about each state of life, we can begin to outline the characteristics of each vocation. And we can also do everything in our power to see that they come to know men and women who are leading these vocations to the full. But our special task as parents in preparing our children for the choice of a vocation is, surely, to show them as fully as we can during all the years of their growth the special characteristics, rewards, and difficulties of our own state of life, the vocation of marriage. For such understanding of this vocation as our own home life can give, should shed light on many aspects of other vocations as well.

The first necessity here is, surely, that we ourselves should be convinced that marriage is a vocation, that is, a Christian way of life planned by God to lead men and women to holiness; and that we should be trying to act accordingly. We must, then, take every means in our power—study, prayer, thought, effort—to convince ourselves that marriage is truly a way of holiness, the way that God has chosen for us.

We must avoid all temptations even to dream about how much holier, healthier, more fully developed, etc., we might have been in some other state—temptations that occasionally beset even the most happily married!—for such dreams bear fruit in our remarks and our outward attitude, and the children may come to feel that we are bitter against home life and marriage as such.

For this purpose, most of us need frequently to re-think and meditate on the fact that marriage has been planned by God as the usual vocation not only of mankind in general, but of the great majority of His own people, the holy nation, the royal priesthood of the Church. And in the light of the sacramental principle of His dealings with us, we can begin to see why He did so. For the way of Christian marriage is beautifully suited to the needs of human creatures who are made up of bodies and souls, and inclined by original and actual sin to make too much of the needs of their bodies.

The essential characteristic of Christian marriage is to lead us by means of the rightful use of our physical powers, as well as our mental and spiritual, to the fullness of knowledge and love and service of God. Our Lord has made marriage a sacrament, the sacrament which is the sign of the union between Christ and His Church for which mankind was made. The whole life of marriage, then, and the act which is characteristic of that life, partake of the sacredness of this union between Christ and His Church, and are means toward our achieving it more and more perfectly.

The great difficulty about the vocation of marriage for many of us today (especially, perhaps, what are called well-educated men and women) is to learn how to appreciate the sacramental value of the whole physical side of married life, not only of the marriage act, but of all the processes of child-bearing and child care and of ordinary household tasks. A great many of us never realized until we were married and had children that human life was so very physical, or that so much time and effort has to be spent on basic physical needs. Our education, our special training, our 'careers' had given us to suppose that our bodies were more or less incidental to our human make-up, rather useful instruments, perhaps, or annoying handicaps, but not to be particularly

107

considered in getting ahead either on earth or toward heaven.

We need, then, to devote thought and prayer to the sacramental significance which God Himself has given to all the basic functions of ordinary married and home life. We need to realize, (at least in the depths of our souls, if not explicitly at the end of Monday morning), that cooking and cleaning and tidying and so on are not merely regrettable necessities in family life, but are meant by God to raise our minds and our hearts to Him, and to be a part of our reasonable service of Him in the vocation of marriage.

If we try to live, then, as if the whole of married life were truly a vocation, our children should grow up with some real idea of what Christian marriage is and is meant to be. They will see it neither as a path of roses, starting at the altar on the wedding morning, along which a young man and woman and a growing train of healthy happy children dance easily up to the gates of heaven, nor as a dreary form of human bondage into which the majority of mankind is trapped by the force of sexual desire and the pressure of society and circumstances. (Nor as the horrid combination of these two pictures which is the impression given by all too many Catholic writers and preachers.)

The children will realize, rather, that Christian marriage rightly lived is the vocation in which we learn to love God and all our neighbors with the love of Christ, primarily by loving one man or woman, and some special children; that it is the vocation of trying to use rightly the things that are seen for the sake of the unseen God; and of helping to build up His kingdom by helping Him to make and form its chosen stones, our children.

Such a view of marriage should also shed light on the other great vocations of Christian life, as they resemble it or differ from it. And it should also help to prevent our children from choosing the wrong vocation, or from choosing the right one for mistaken or warped motives. For one thing, they should not be easily misled into thinking that holiness and the full service of God and neighbor can only be sought in the priesthood or the religious life, for they will have learned that these are the purposes of every Christian life.

Nor will they think that the desire to spend themselves and their talents for God can be satisfied only in the priesthood or the dedicated single life. They will not think that marriage or 'ordinary life' is meant to be an easy way to heaven, so that they would be likely to refuse a real call to the priesthood or religious life or the dedicated single life on the grounds of hardship or difficulty. Nor will there be, please God, any of that shrinking from sex or mistaken valuation of its pleasures which can so complicate both the choice of a vocation and its fulfillment.

And so the children should be at least comparatively free to choose their own vocation and life work in accordance with God's will. They should be free to put the question in the right form: What does God want me to do? rather than: What do I want to do, like to do, think I can get ahead in, etc. And they should then be free to use all the proper means to find the right answer to that question—their own knowledge of themselves and their capabilities, circumstances, the advice of authorities, and, above all, prayer and the search to conform themselves to God's will.

Then, even if they do not feel sure of what God wants of them when they finish their education, even if they have to feel their way, to try various kinds of work, to take the first step towards more than one vocation, they will be sure that God does have a vocation for them, and that if they keep asking and seeking and knocking, in His own best time He will show them what it is.

1. What is the meaning of the term "Christian vocation"? Does the term have meaning only for those who enter the religious life?

2. What are the chief aims of life according to secular standards?

3. What is the work of Christ's priests?

4. What are the characteristics of a call to the life of a single Christian in the world?

5. What, according to the author, are the most important aspects of Christian marriage?

Discussion topics

1. Discuss the author's statement that "Young people are normally heroic-minded." To what extent does the secular standard of security and pleasure and ease affect modern youth? How can we rebuild the mentality that the various Christian vocations are challenging and exciting and truly satisfying?

2. List the various factors that seem to be productive of religious vocations in families. What can be done to increase the number of religious vocations?

3. Discuss marriage as a vocation. What does the author mean by stating that we must learn "to appreciate the sacramental value of the whole physical side of married life."

4. Discuss the role of parents in aiding their children to choose the right vocation, and for the right reasons. Is there any danger that children will be poorly prepared for their vocation even if they have the right motive?

5. Reflect on the dignity of the priesthood. What practices and attitudes on the part of parents help to build a respectful and balanced understanding of the clergy in the minds of the children? What practices and attitudes may lead to critical and unappreciative ideas about the function of the priesthood?

9 REDEEMING THE TIME

The irreligious character of modern civilization is, certainly, shown most clearly in the kind of daily, weekly, yearly schedules which it tends to impose on us. Consider the daily program of a typical American family: father rushes off to work by train or bus or subway or car; the children hurry to school; mother hurries to get all her housework and marketing finished; as soon as anyone gets home again, or finishes what he is doing, he begins to think about the next pressing demand of social or economic life. How little is such a program of hurrying and worrying designed to foster a sense of the presence of God, how little to develop the religious potentialities of daily life, or growth in Christian living!

Or consider the plan of the typical American family's week: the strain of the five working days, the weekend filled with odd jobs, violent amusements, and the relaxation of exhaustion. What relation has this to the Christian idea of the week? Or, again the typical yearly round: school begins for the children, all sorts of activities begin for the parents, the Thanksgiving turkey, the Christmas rush, Valentine's Day, winter, Easter bunnies and chocolate, spring, end of school, plans for a vacation, etc. How can years that concentrate our attention on such non-essentials do anything but hinder gradual normal growth in Christian living for either parents or children?

Here, surely, is one of our greatest problems as Christian parents: how can we give our children the idea of a fundamentally Christian pattern for a day, a week, or a year, tied as most of us are and must be in so many ways to the almost completely secular timing of the world around us? We cannot simply take the pattern of a monastery's schedule, nor can we impose a design of living taken from another time and place, however Christian and desirable such designs, in themselves, might be. For we need to give our children at least the outline of a pattern of life which at once is Christian, and of our own time and place.

The only practical way to go about such a task is, surely, under the guidance of the Church, to think out the purposes for which God gave us days and weeks and years as units of time in our lives. The Church clearly teaches us, by her own official schedule of daily and weekly prayer and services, of yearly feasts and fasts, that the fundamental time-units of our lives are meant to have a sacramental meaning and a sacramental purpose. If we understand this sacramental meaning and purpose, then, we shall be able to plan how again under the guidance of the Church, we can make the most Christian ordering possible under our own circumstances of the days and weeks and years of our family living.

To begin with the day, then. The Church has always seen in each dawn the image of our Lord's resurrection and of our rising to true life with Him. Each day's Mass, in which the great Action of our redemption is re-presented for us to share in, is the focus, the vital center of the day, radiating its light and force through all the Hours of the Church's prayer, with Vespers as its evening shadow, a sacrifice of praise. And Compline shows us that each night's sleep is meant to be a rehearsal for our death in Christ, teaching us how, with contrition and hope, to commend ourselves and all our work and care, with our Lord dying on the Cross into the loving hands of the Father.

Each day, in other words, is meant to be an image of the *whole* Christian life, and is meant to help us toward that perfect conformation to our Lord and to His redeeming action for which we all were made, and for which we were given the fundamental powers at our Baptism.

What does this mean for our daily family schedule? First of all, surely, that we should try to see each new day as an image of the resurrection, a rising to newness of life in Christ, to try to live more perfectly to God, in the strength of Christ, than we did yesterday. Children naturally begin each new day quite afresh; they seldom have conscious hangovers from yesterday's mistakes and faults. Let us, then, in spite of our own morning fatigue and irritation and the complications of getting a family started on the day's routine, try to show the children that each new day is a gift from God, that we want to thank Him for it, that we want to offer everything in it to Him with our Lord's offering at Mass, and ask His help to use the day all for Him.

Some sort of family morning prayers are usually possible just before breakfast, at least while the children are small enough to have the same schedules and be able to eat breakfast together. Let us take this opportunity to give them a pattern of morning prayer for their whole lives, not simply a routine "Our Father" and "Hail Mary," but one which will contain praise, joy, offering, prayers for help and protection.[1]

Let us also occasionally try to show the children, when occasion offers during the day's work or play, that our morning offering (or, obviously, our taking part in the Mass) means a willing consecration of the whole day, that we meant to share in our Lord's work during the day, and now should not be taking our offering back by complaints and whining and rebellion.

Then, however we spend the morning hours, there is usually a pause somewhere around noontime, at least for lunch. The Angelus is the age-old sanctioned form of mid-day prayer for the laity, recalling the whole mystery of our salvation, bringing us back to a moment's peace in the presence of God. While the children are small enough to have lunch at home, and on weekends and during holidays with the whole family, let us, then establish the Angelus as a family habit; again, as far as possible, not as routine prayer but as an opportunity to be reminded of what the whole day is for.

Finally, somewhere in the course of the late afternoon and evening, some sort of family "evening song" or praise of God is surely the Christian order. Most families meet at the supper table. Let us take this opportunity for some *short* psalm (Psalm 116, for instance) or hymn, or prayer of praise as part of grace before or after the meal.

And, while the children are young enough to have a set bed time and to say night prayers in common, let us give them a pattern of night prayers which will include all the essentials: a sorrow for what has been done wrong and

---

[1] A very good form of morning offering for children, and for morning prayers, is to be found in that excellent child's prayerbook, *Glory to God,* by Dorothy Coddington (W. H. Sadlier & Co.).

115

prayer for forgiveness, commending one's soul and all that one is and has into the hands of the Father with our Lord's dying on the Cross, in the hope of rising with Him to new life and strength tomorrow.

The basic plan of a Christian day, then, would seem to be: getting up with hope and joy and thanks (in our wills at least); offering ourselves (by taking part in the Mass or, when this is not possible, by a morning offering) to share in our Lord's work and suffering and death during the day; recalling ourselves to this fundamental purpose of our day's work and play and asking God's help to carry it out, at least once during the day; and, in the evening, praising God for His goodness, and for enabling us by His grace to make our life and work of some real use and purpose; and, before we go to sleep, handing ourselves over once more to Him in contrition and hope, with Christ our Lord.

Surely these essentials would not overcrowd a family's timetable, but would rather serve to weld all the items in the day's schedule into a more peaceful and purposeful unity. The first step, perhaps, would be for the parents themselves consciously to try to mould their days on such a pattern; then, if there are older children, to discuss the whole purpose of a day with them and see how they think it should be achieved. Then anything "new" would not be just another thing to do, but seem part of a plan.

With small children, a new season is always a good excuse for starting a new "practice," like a psalm at supper time, or a new form of morning or night prayers. The beginning of Advent or Lent, for instance, gives a fine chance to rearrange prayers and prayer-times to achieve their purpose more perfectly. (For the sake of avoiding routine, if nothing else, prayers of all kinds should surely be varied by season as much as possible.)

And when we have established these basic essentials of a Christian day in our family living, then would seem to be the time to consider how much more in the way of communal or private prayer, divine office, reading, etc., should be part of the day's plan, what would truly help each of us and the family as a whole, to conform ourselves and to be conformed by God's grace each day to the image and action of Christ.[1]

The Christian week begins with Sunday, the "day of the Lord," a "little Easter," a day of triumph in our Lord's triumph over death by His death, a day of entering by hope into the happiness and peace of eternal life which He won for us.[2] In Sunday's Mass, the whole Christian people come together to hear about the mystery of our redemption; to offer themselves to be united with it; to re-live it with Christ offering Himself through the hands of the priest and to receive His own life and strength to unite them with Him and with each other; to make ready for another week of carrying out His redemptive work in their daily lives.

The weekdays following Sunday reflect and radiate its special light and grace in their praise and prayers, until Friday brings us to remember particularly the day of our Lord's death by the prescribed rule of abstinence, and Saturday begins to end one week and to prepare for a new Sunday, a new beginning in Christ.

For most of us, alas, such a program does not *seem* at all like the actual weeks we live through. But, if we concen-

[1] The *Manual of Prayers* prepared by the Precious Blood Sisters of O'Fallon, Mo., is an inexpensive booklet containing a good variety of psalms and other prayers arranged for seasonal use.

[2] It is well worthwhile to ponder the implications of the fact that Sunday is considered by some Fathers of the Church not to be merely the first in a series of weekdays, but rather the *eighth* day, outside of the seven days of ordinary time, partaking in the perfection and time-less-ness of eternity.

trate on the essentials, we can do a great deal to make this pattern of a Christian week mould the pattern of our weeks, so that they may become more nearly in fact the Christian weeks we want them to be.

We need, first of all, to aim towards making Sunday a day of "newness," a day of Christian happiness, a day of re-creative rest, all centered around the Sunday Mass; and we need in some way to make the remainder of the week take its start and tone from Sunday's light and grace, until towards the end of the week, we begin to prepare for another new beginning.

Toward this sense of "newness," all the week-end cleaning and preparations (which most of us do in any case) need only to be undertaken not just because they have to be done sometime, but for the sake of the Lord's Day. And, perhaps, if we can manage to do such things more in the spirit of joyful preparation for a feast, the children will take their due share less unwillingly. Towards making Sunday a day of happiness and re-creative rest, we can also try to make it the day on which, more than any other, we do special things, or have the sort of friends to visit, or be visited by, whom the whole family enjoys.

To center Sunday, and so the whole week, on Sunday Mass is, certainly, as things are now both in the set-up of family and parish life today, the most difficult part of re-making a Christian week. Sunday Mass just does not *seem* like the focus of our lives. But, of course, we know that it *is*. But there is no use in not admitting to ourselves the obvious fact that it is only in the very deepest recesses of our faith that we can center our lives, and each week of our lives, in the "hurry and get 'em out" type of Sunday Mass that is, due to many historical circumstances, still prevalent in so many parishes today—a type of celebration in which the Mass itself is treated as sacred magic, at which the people "have" to be present, but which they cannot and need not understand.

It is difficult enough, heaven knows, even when one is free to use one's Missal and to take silent part in such a Mass, to realize that one has, in fact, taken part in the greatest Action of a Christian's individual and social life. But when one has to go to such a Mass with children, one can only pray that the Holy Spirit will somehow give them a sense of its wonder and the fruit of its graces, in spite of the hustle and bustle and general unsacredness of most of the sounds and sights all round.

But there are hopeful indications in many places today of the action of the Holy Spirit working in the Church to remedy this situation, to find the best ways and means to make the whole celebration of the Mass once more a meaningful sign to us of its supernatural reality and action, and to educate us to appreciate this sign and to take our full and rightful part in the celebration. The Encyclical on the Sacred Liturgy teaches us what our part in the Mass should be; the same Encyclical and the official instructions and the text of the restored Easter Vigil indicate that the highest authorities in the Church want everything possible done to make it easy for us to take that part as fully as we can.

While, therefore, we are doing whatever we can to cooperate with our pastors in promoting fuller and more intelligent participation in the Mass in our parish, while we are also doing whatever we can, with our pastor and neighbors, to make Sunday Mass less of a chore and more of an opportunity to worship for other people with families—what can we do at home? We might try, for example, to find time on Saturday not only for confession as needed, but also for teaching the small children something about the Mass. On Sunday itself we might find some time to read, if possible, the whole chapter of the Gospel from which the Sunday's gospel is taken, or the Old Testament reading for that Sunday, or the psalms of the Mass. Above all—and this we could certainly all do without adding anything to our schedules!—we can try to speak and act as if we realized the enormous privilege it is to take part in Sunday Mass, never as if it were a chore or merely a duty.

Throughout the week, also, we could remind ourselves and the children, as occasion offers, of the consequences of taking part in Sunday's Mass. As a little girl once said: "You offer the whole week to God and you mustn't take it back." Where possible we could continue the Sunday readings and prayers, as part of our own family study and prayer life.

Then Friday's abstinence will take its place not as another chore (or as a badge of loyal Catholicism!) but as a sharing by obedience and some slight deprivation in our Lord's obedience unto death. And Saturday will begin to become less of a day of no school, dentists, shopping and amusements, more a day of happy preparation for another Sunday.

In such simple ways, without adding anything to our schedule, we can begin to re-fashion our weeks, however hectic they may be, more nearly to the Christian design. And so we shall be giving our children a basic Christian pattern of days and weeks, which they can carry out in their future lives under any circumstances, and a basically Christian way of thinking about days and weeks, which they themselves can develop, with the grace of God, each according to his own vocation, towards the building-up, if God wills, of a truly Christian culture.

In the same way, we can study the essential purpose and design of the Church's year, and of each season and feast, and see how the already existing elements in our lives can be used or adapted to achieve this purpose, to carry out this design. Then we can see what we need to add, and what would be wise and making for family happiness to add or adapt to our family observances at each feast or season out of the rich treasure house of age-old customs, and those developed by other families today.[1]

The purpose of the feast of Christmas, for example, (considering the Christmas-Epiphany season as one great feast) is, ultimately, to rehearse and prepare us for the final coming of Christ in glory at the end of the world. Through Advent, the Church rehearses the preparation of the whole human race, and of the Chosen People in particular, for the historic coming of Christ. For our Lord's birth at Bethlehem, in the grand design of God, was only the beginning of His coming in His kingdom, in the Church, which will be completed and shown in its full glory when He comes again at the end of the world.

Now it is by our active love, in Christ, for each other that we will be judged on that final day of His coming. We prepare most perfectly to welcome Him then in His glory by welcoming Him now in His least brethren. The Christmas Masses, in the real order of sacramental grace, and also all the time-honored ways of picturing and representing our Lord's historic birth in Bethlehem, are, ultimately, for the purpose of awakening our gratitude and love for Christ's coming to us as our Head and our Redeemer; so that we will serve Him better now, in each other, and so, all together, be the readier to welcome Him when He returns in glory.

[1] For this purpose, see particularly Therese Mueller's booklets, *Family Life in Christ* (Liturgical Press) and *Our Children's Year of Grace* (Pio Decimo Press); Msgr. Hellriegel's article in *The Family in Christ* (Proceedings of the 1946 Liturgical Week, Elsberry, Mo.); and Mrs. Florence Berger's *Cooking For Christ* (National Catholic Rural Life Conference, Des Moines, Ia.).

All the business, then of Christmas giving and of keeping in touch with our friends all over the world by cards and presents (activities which so easily become merely tiresome and commercial) could be re-thought-out in this light, and, without omitting any of our real duties and obligations, be made a true and happy service of Christ in each other. What still survives of the real "Christmas spirit" (and surely there is more than pessimists admit, even in department stores) is actually a joy in carefree and happy giving beyond the call of duty; since God's Son became Man, when we give to each other we now truly give to Him, and in the gifts we receive from each other, we receive gifts from His love. By re-aligning, then, in this light, our Christmas customs and Christmas doing, including all the preparations, we can accomplish a great deal truly to "put Christ back into Christmas," or, better, to let Him remake our Advent and Christmas according to His own original plan.

The ideal is to orient every element in our daily lives—prayer, study, work, play—toward the celebration of each feast or season, to allow the special light and grace and vitality of each feast and season to permeate every aspect of our lives. (The word "celebrate" comes from a Latin root meaning "to frequent," to gather in crowds. So we should gather ourselves and our lives round the Church's feasts and fasts if we are to celebrate them fully.)

Even from the merely human point of view, to make our humdrum lives into a succession of celebrations of different kinds would, surely, give them the color and variety and interest for which every human being naturally hungers. And since the feasts and fasts of the Church have been planned by the Holy Spirit for our education and growth in Christ's life, the color and variety and interest which they give our lives is not merely human, but also divine.

No parent can help thinking about all the crimes and follies committed by very young people today, sometimes even murders. And when we study the published investigations of such crimes, we see that they were committed largely because the boys were bored, because they saw no real purpose or interest in their present or future lives and had been taught no legitimate ways of finding interest and variety in the course of daily living and so had recourse to drinking, dope, and unsafe driving in an unending search for easy "thrills." Such considerations force us to pray for our own children, and all children. And they also should urge us to try to guide our children toward the never-failing Source of all the true interest and excitement of life, and toward making use of all the marvelous means He has given us for making our daily lives truly interesting and full of variety.

The yearly course of the liturgy offers us also to make the "terrible round" of our daily duties more purposeful and more interesting. For each year we are given a new chance to think about the great sacraments whose outward signs are taken from the ordinary materials and actions of daily life.

Lent and Easter time offer us the opportunity to think about Baptism, to guide our own and our children's thoughts to the whole idea of water in God's plan, of what it does for us in daily life, of how God has used it in the course of history, of how our Lord used it, and of how in His name the Church now uses it as the medium of our rebirth in Christ.

Holy Thursday, Pentecost, give us the chance to think about Confirmation, to consider why our Lord chose oil for the matter of this sacrament of maturity and activity for Christ, why it is used in Ordinations and for Extreme Unction. So we can begin to appreciate from above down, so to speak, the ultimate value and purpose of all our family washing and cleaning and waxing and polishing and tidying and decorating; we can begin to see all these actions, so full of drudgery and fatigue, as means of raising our thoughts and desires to the wonders of God's life as well as means of achieving the final fruit of all these wonders, the life of the redeemed in heaven.

In the same way, each Holy Thursday, each feast of Corpus Christi, (as well as every Sunday of the year) gives us the opportunity to think about and appreciate the significance of the Bread and Wine of the holy Eucharist, and to make our own use of food and drink more of a means of appreciating that true Food of our Christian lives, of preparing us to take part in the banquet and in the eternal feast of heaven of which it is the pledge.

An element of the greatest importance in this "redeeming of the time" in our homes, and in fact in every aspect of Christian life and education, is the element of silence, quiet, the necessary substratum of peace. This does not mean, of course, that we should aim at making a house full of lively children as quiet as a convent. But it does mean that we should try to eliminate unnecessary and purposeless noises from our homes. Children have to shout, of course, but not all the time, or everywhere; and they need a reasonable amount of quietness every day for the sake of their nerves as well as their souls. Let us try to give them the sense, then, that silence and quiet are quite normal, and that sounds are to be made for a purpose. (Few things, for example, are less calculated to foster growth of the Christian spirit than a radio or TV set which is left turned on and simply allowed to make noise that nobody really attends to, but which prevents anyone from paying full attention to anything else.)

Real private or communal prayer, happy, intelligent conversation, and all kinds of joyful noise to the Lord are the fruit of some real silence and the chance to think. The most active children want and need time to be alone, quiet in which to think their own thoughts, silence in which to "just think." Privacy and quiet often seem some of the most expensive of luxuries today; but let us try to give our children as much of them as is possible. And then we will find it much easier to cooperate with God's grace in instilling into both speech and silence, necessary and happy noise and quiet, the spirit of Christian peace.

But, of course, all these means for sanctifying days and weeks and years, all the framework of prayers and customs and the orientation of work and play toward the life of the Church, need to be vivified and made fruitful by the Holy Spirit, by the personal intercourse of each member of the family with our Lord and His Father and the Holy Spirit, with our Lady and the saints and his own guardian angel. Our part, here, is, above all, prayer that God will show Himself to each of our children and attract them to Himself as He wishes; and, of course, we know that He is far more anxious to do so than we could be.

But we can do something to cooperate with His action by encouraging the children to talk simply and naturally to God about their joys and sorrows or troubles, not trying to tell them what to say but suggesting subjects for conversation. Again, we can encourage their cultivating the acquaintance of their guardian angels, "Why not ask your Angel what would be the best thing to do about this . . . " And we can avoid, above all, the error of only suggesting prayer when the children have been naughty, or as a means of backing up our own whims, "Now you tell God you are sorry you have been such a bad boy . . .," and the like. When a child has been bad, and has realized the error of

125

his ways, then is the time to suggest, "Don't you want to tell God now that you are sorry . . .," but also, on happy occasions, "Don't you want to thank God for this lovely day . . ." [1]

If we are trying to sacramentalize our daily lives, to live the life of the Church inwardly and as outwardly also as circumstances permit, then the course of each day and week and year should offer its own opportunities to teach the children as much as they are capable of learning about God, about the truths of the faith. The guide in general to what the children are capable of understanding and absorbing is, here again, mainly the children's own interest and span of attention.

If the children are attending a Catholic school and having regular instruction in religion, our job is to try to make sure that the instruction becomes concrete and vital in the children's lives. If we are solely responsible for their formal religious education, we must see to it that our own preferences do not cause us to omit some essential element of faith or morals, and also that the children finally obtain the exactly worded and systematic knowledge of their faith which they will need as part of their equipment.

But our main task, in any case, is so to present the truths of faith to the children's developing minds and hearts that the children not only *assent* to them, but begin truly to *consent* to them, to incorporate them into their daily living.

Here again, obviously we should use above all the means used by God Himself in His instruction of the human race in the mysteries of His life and of our incorporation into it, that is, Holy Scripture and the liturgy. God did not speak

[1] On this topic, and many others sketched in this book, see the excellent and more detailed treatment in *Ourselves and Our Children* by Mary Reed Newland (Kennedy).

to His People in the Old Testament in syllogisms but in figures and types, and in the very events of their history. And all this is now, as St. Paul tells us, "for our instruction."

Our Lord did not speak even to His apostles in a logically ordered series of lectures, but in parables and stories and, above all, by His own life and actions. So beneath and all around the systematic teaching of the truths of faith, let us give our children their inheritance of Holy Scripture, the mental climate of the Bible and the liturgy, which is, precisely, the climate which fosters the Christian sacramental spirit.

It is by means of loving familiarity with the Bible and with the liturgy that we best learn how to look at all creation so that it will raise our minds and hearts to God and to the mysteries of our redemption, that we learn how to use created things for the love of God. The Bible and the liturgy are the means of religious instruction which satisfy all the complex requirements of our complex human nature; they are truly *incarnational,* because they are the manifestation of the Incarnate Word. They are inexhaustible sources of growth in the knowledge and love of God, and nothing can replace them in the Christian life.

If, by the grace of the Holy Spirit, we are to any degree successful in our task of thus "redeeming the time" in our homes, then each day and week and year of our family life and our children's growth will contribute something towards giving them the basic pattern of Christian life on earth, the pattern of living, suffering and dying with Christ in the strength of His already accomplished victory, working with Him to bring every human being into the scope of that victory, looking forward to sharing fully with all our brothers and fellow members of the mystical Body in the fruits of that victory forever in heaven.

127

One result of such a training should be that the children do not look forward as a right to lives of security, ease, earthly comfort and happiness, but rather to lives of struggle, work, hardship, monotony—and joy in Christ.

Another result should be that they are not afraid of the thought of death. No human being, of course, can help that natural fear of death from which our Lord Himself suffered in the Garden. But we Christians should certainly not share in the modern unrealistic avoidance of the whole idea of death, which results in hiding from dying people the fact of their nearness to death, and in obscuring the obvious fact that we are all going to die and should make plans for it.

We should take the opportunities offered, then, by the thought of our Lord's own death, by All Souls' Day, prayers for the dead, burials and funeral Masses to show the children that death is meant to be the crowning, climactic act of life on earth, the act by which we finally can complete the offering of ourselves to God with Christ, the dying to sin and living to God which has been the main effort of our whole lives.

We can show the children also, beginning when they are quite young, that the only real horror of death comes from sin, so that they should pray for the dying and the dead, and begin to look forward and prepare themselves for the hour of their own death. And we can teach them above all that death is the gateway to true life, the door to our true home in heaven.

One of the safest and most beautiful ways of teaching the children about death is to use the Church's own prayers for the dying as a text. For the wisdom of the Church has constructed these prayers in a perfect balance of true fear of God and holy hope.[1]

[1] These prayers are contained in *A Manual of Prayers* for the use of the Catholic laity, prepared by order of the Third Plenary Council of Baltimore

And if we take such means to give the children some understanding of death from year to year, we will be preparing both them and ourselves for death in our own family, or among those who are dear to us. We shall, then, when death visits our own house, be better able to make it clear to the children that we are not sorry that our beloved is on his way to the fullness of true life with Christ in God; what we are mourning is our own loss; what we are praying for is that his soul may go straight to heaven and that we may have the courage to go on living in this valley of tears without him.

And, again, as we try to found our daily lives on the true Christian pattern, we will be giving our children the basis for a realistic and Christian idea of history. They will have a defense for the future against that false optimism of our times which sees progress as inevitable ("If thus and so does not come about, Western civilization will end. Therefore it must come about . . ." You can find such a line of argument in almost any speech or pronouncement about the future of this country, of the U.N. or what-have-you), and the false pessimism and despair into which such opinion is so easily transformed at the sight of actual historical trends and events.

Our children will, rather, grow up to see all history as the struggle between good and evil, in which Christ will be finally victorious, as the process by which the dough of mankind is being imperceptibly leavened by the action of Christ in His Church. They will realize that what is visible to us now is mainly the struggle, the battle, often the temporary outward defeat of Christ's forces, but that victory is assured,

(Kenedy & Sons, N.Y.); it is a book which no family should be without, since it contains the ceremonies for administering the sacraments, the essentials of what Christians should believe and do, and much more besides.

that, though we cannot see it, the Kingdom of God is actually being built up and will finally come down from heaven "prepared as a Bride adorned for her husband."

Whatever catastrophe the future may bring, then, our children will have the assurance of Christian hope, renewed every morning, every Sunday, every Easter time, renewed above all with every reception of holy Communion, that Christ has already overcome the world, and that they can overcome it in and with Him. And they will have learned not so much to dread as to look forward to the Coming of Christ, whether in their own death or at the end of the world, and to pray the true prayer of Christian expectation: "Amen. Come, Lord Jesus!"

DISCUSSION topics

1. How is Sunday viewed by the average American? What suggestions can be offered for a return to "keeping holy" the Lord's Day? What practical measures within the family should be used to emphasize the dignity and importance of Sunday? How do we spend our time? How do we dress? How do we prepare the meal and the house? Would a pagan notice a marked difference between the Sunday order of the day in a Catholic home as compared with non-Christian citizens?

2. What is the significance of the Christmas and Epiphany cycle of the Church year? What can be done realistically to "restore Christ in Christmas"? How much of the reform can take place within our own family circle? Does the story of Santa Claus interfere with the child's grasp of the true meaning of Christmas?

3. Review the author's suggestions for a Christian day. How could this plan be adapted to meet individual needs of our own families? What are the best and what are the most difficult times for having family prayer?

4. Discuss possibilities for groups of Catholic couples cooperating on a religious program to intensify the spiritual life of its members. What are the opportunities for having a family day of recollection? of making family retreats? of starting Catholic Action groups for married couples? of family Communion Sundays? of increasing participation at Holy Mass?

5. Make a comparison of the amount of time and energy spent by family members in reading daily newspapers, listening to the news over the radio, and reading popular magazines, with the amount of time given to reading the Bible or spiritual books. If children can learn dozens of "hit of the week" songs during the course of the year, would it be possible for them to learn (and chant aloud) some of the Psalms?

1. What does the author suggest as a prayer pattern for each day and what suggestions are made for family use of this pattern?

2. What is the significance of Sunday in the Church's week? of Saturday? of Friday?

3. What is the meaning of the Lent and Easter cycle in the Church year —and how can the Christian mother tie the liturgical spirit of this season in with her housecleaning?

4. Why should there be periods of silence in the home?

5. What is the Christian attitude toward death?

10 sex education

The question of sex education has certainly become a distinct and anxious problem for parents today, more so, probably, than at any other time in the history of mankind. But the chief, though not the only, reason why it has become such a problem, is, surely, that for the first time in the history of mankind a widespread culture has been developed with no integrated view of reality into which the complex fact of "sex" might be fitted. Every other great culture has had such a view, and, as a result, sex was not thought of as an isolated phenomenon in human life, but in some way organically related to forces above and below man himself— at the least to his flocks and fields below him, and his gods above. But the great majority of people today have no way of interpreting either the fact of sex itself, or its many-sided repercussions in individual and social life. They see it in isolation, either as a rather distasteful biological device for propagating the human race, or as a mere means to pleasure, or as an end in itself that serves one's personal needs for self-realization and self-development.

Or else, under the pressure of the obvious fact that sex does have echoes and repercussions on all levels of human life, people come to accept the idea that an understanding of the role of sex in human life is actually the master key to understanding the make-up of human beings and the phenomena of human behavior. In any case, it is no wonder that people find it embarrassing to teach children the "facts of life," since the teachers themselves realize, at least dimly, that they are in the presence of a mystery, but do not know just where the mystery lies.

But we Catholics have no need to share in this embarrassment. Our faith teaches us that God designed everything created to be in some way or another a means of teaching us about Himself, and a means of leading us toward Himself. In particular, we know that in His primal designing of man's body and soul, God had in mind—to use human language—the final purpose for which He was bringing mankind into existence, a supernatural union of life and love with Himself.

He therefore designed man and woman so that their physical union would at once be the expression and the image of their spiritual union of life and love in marriage; and so that this whole psycho-physical and spiritual union of marriage would be the image, the foreshowing of our union with Christ. And, in the marvelous ordering of His Wisdom, God designed the physical union of man and woman as the means whereby human beings could cooperate with the creative power of His own Love to bring new human beings into existence. And He planned the whole of marriage and home life to be the first means whereby human beings are completely formed, taught and trained to achieve the purpose of their existence.

Thus God has wonderfully designed us so that the means whereby His creative love brings all the generations of mankind into being for the purpose of sharing His life and happiness in love for all eternity—this means should itself be the image of that final purpose of His love for us in Christ.[1]

Catholic doctrine also teaches us that, when our first parents turned away from God's love in the disobedience of original sin, this wonderful power of procreation at once showed the tragic and disastrous effects of sin's disordering of man and nature. This great force in man and woman, designed to give them the glory of cooperating freely and intelligently with the infinite Force of God's own creative Love, now was no longer completely under their own control; it became a blind and often uncontrollable power leading to confusion and further sin.

The history of mankind shows in how many ways men have misunderstood and misused and degraded and perverted this most wonderful of all man's natural powers. But God's primal blessing was never taken away from human marriage; this power of man's still served God's purpose, though blindly and unwillingly, bringing into existence the generations of mankind down through the ages, so that Christ should be

[1] "O God, who by Thy mighty power hast made all things where before there was nothing; who, having framed and put in order the first kinds of all creatures, didst constitute woman as a helpmate for man made to Thine image, a helpmate, therefore, who should never be separated from him; fashioning her in such a way that woman's body took its origin from man's flesh, and teaching thereby that since it pleased Thee to construct her body from his, it is never right that their union be sundered . . .

"O God, who hast consecrated the marriage union by a hidden and sacred design so exceedingly great that in the marriage covenant Thou dost foreshow the Mystery of Christ and the Church . . .

"O God, who dost join woman to man, and give to that primal society the blessing which alone was not taken away in punishment for original sin nor by the doom of the Flood . . ." (From the Blessing given during the Nuptial Mass.)

135

born and redeem the race of which He made Himself a member.

And now, in Christ our Lord, God has revealed His whole plan to us; in the Church, Christ's Body, He gives us the grace to cooperate with that plan according to our vocation; and, by the sacrament of marriage, each Christian marriage is actually formed on the image of Christ's union with His Church, and married people are given the graces to make their married lives develop and grow through the years in conformity with this pattern, thus intelligently and lovingly using the marriage act and marriage in free accord with God's designs.

Catholic teaching, then, explicitly shows us that the facts of sex are most intimately interwoven with God's whole plan for mankind (as every pagan culture rightly suspected without knowing the plan). We parents surely owe our children the truly integrated and integrating "sex education" which only Catholics can give, that sees the facts about sex and the implications of these facts in the whole context of human life and destiny, in the light of Christ's truth and by the power of His grace.

The main thing is, surely, that we ourselves should take whatever means we find necessary—study, prayer, thought—to relate all the various aspects of sex to our knowledge of God's whole plan and of its working-out in history, and to do so in such a thorough way, with the help of God, that in neither our thoughts nor our actions or reactions will there remain any clammy wisps of the fog of Manichaeism which, in one or more of its myriad forms, has penetrated so much modern thinking and feeling.

Then we shall be in a position to give our children the facts of sex in their proper context, and, as need arises during all the years of their development, help them to understand

and to deal with the repercussions of the facts in their own lives and in the lives of others. If we ourselves are quite sure of the place of sex in God's plans, then specific information about where babies come from will fit naturally at the proper time into our day-by-day training in knowledge and admiration of God's workmanship as shown in the whole range of created things.

Right ideas about purity, modesty, chastity will fit naturally into our daily training in respect for oneself and others as marvels of God's making and re-making, children of God, members and co-workers of Christ, temples of the Holy Spirit. The warnings which we shall need to give the children about the possibilities of misusing sexual powers, and natural and supernatural precautions against such misuse, will fit naturally into our whole teaching about the consequences of the Fall and the Redemption in our own lives.

In the same way, all the other aspects of the whole training which we are trying to give the children will contribute toward their gaining the true sacramental appreciation of sex. The familiarity with nature which is a normal part of children's education, the care of gardens and pets, the link-up of all scientific information with admiration and praise for God's designs, all this will give the children the background for an appreciation of God's even more wonderful designing of themselves and of all their powers unto His glory.

The training we try to give them in acquiring skills of mind and body and in striving for skillful and charitable workmanship in everything they do will prepare the way for their instruction, if and when they come to be married, in the art of married life and the art of the marriage act itself. Again, all our training in ordering the whole of life to the loving service of Christ in others should help them to

137

distinguish true love and true affection from counterfeits, both in themselves and others.

And, above all, our attempts to live the life of the Church, to give the children true familiarity with the liturgy and Holy Scripture, should be a most powerful means of truly Catholic education in sex, as in all the other fundamentals of life.

Thus, with the help of God, we should be able to give the children by the time they reach maturity, the essentials of Christian sex education, so that they may be able to assimilate and deal with the manifold expressions and repercussions of sex in human behavior as the vocation of each child may require. They should have, first of all, the makings of a happy and humorous appreciation of their own manhood or womanhood, of the special flavor it gives to life and to all human relations, of its special possibilities for full human and Christian living, of its special dangers and difficulties whether physical, emotional, mental or spiritual, and of the special place it enables one to take in the whole work of the Church of God.

They should have, also, a positive love of the virtue of purity as being the splendor of the right, undeflected ordering of one's powers to the love of God; and the correlative horror of impurity as the spoiling, misuse, violation of what is God's and meant for God.

They should have, again, the growing realization that the vast possibilities of holiness and horror, of happiness and tragedy, to be found in human love and union are the effects of the mystery of sanctity—the mystery of marriage as designed by God—which is the proper framework, fruit and ultimate purpose of the love and union of man and woman.

In this light, they should also see that only in marriage

and according to God's laws for marriage, can our procreative powers be used as God meant and designed them to be. And, therefore, the use of them outside of marriage, or their abuse in marriage, cannot be expected to result in joy, happiness, or, ultimately, even pleasure.

In the light of true appreciation for the mystery of Christian marriage, the children should have a correlative appreciation of the even higher mystery and vocation of consecrated virginity, the inspired dedication of the whole and the best of oneself directly to Christ.

And, again, such a truly Christian sex education which is given as part of a general sacramental outlook and training, should give our children the ability to understand the reasons for the chief emotional and spiritual overtones which inevitably accompany the idea of sex, and to attribute these overtones to that aspect of sex to which they rightly belong and not to some other.

Every normal person feels a sense of mystery in connection with sex. But there is nothing unusually mysterious about the anatomical and physiological facts of human reproduction in themselves; the mystery lies in the wonder of the effect of human reproduction, a new human being; in the intimate interweaving of God's design of human procreation and marriage with His highest and most sacred plans for His glory and our eternal happiness; in the marvellous release, which follows on self-donation, of our powers of knowing and loving and of self-realization; and in the horror of sin which can degrade and pervert such a wonderful power to the services of evil.

Again, every normal person feels that there is something humorous about sex, that both the marriage act and marriage have many funny aspects together with their essential sacredness. The true basis for this feeling is, of course, that here above all God does not want us to mistake the image for the Reality, the temporal and human foreshadowing of eternal happiness in love for that happiness itself. And so He made the image, the foreshadow as crude, as humorously incongruous with the Reality which it signifies, as His Wisdom deemed necessary to keep us from mistaking the means for the end. A rightly-ordered sense of humor about sex and marriage is, therefore, a proper reaction to the whole range of Reality. But because of the disorder wrought by original sin, this sense of humor is all too easily turned into something puerile or really perverted; it joins hands with the sense of disgust which properly applies only to the misuse of sex; and leads to that degraded attitude made up of giggles and feelings of guilt which is so common in our country today.

In all these matters, then, the whole form and spirit of the training we are trying to give the children should provide them with the basis for rightly interpreting their own and other people's emotions and feelings about sex, and for continually rectifying their own by the help of God's grace in accordance with the light of Christian wisdom.

The actual facts about sex—anatomical, biological, moral and theological—we should be able to give simply and matter-of-factly as their age and circumstances and general awareness of reality dictate, avoiding both the dangers of overwhelming them with information which they do not yet need and cannot digest, and of failing to have given them sufficient information for their needs and circumstances. We surely need to pray for the guidance of the Holy Spirit here, as everywhere else, and for the protection of our children from danger that we could not foresee or forestall.

Otherwise the safest guide in most cases would seem to be what a child himself really wants to know at any given moment. The arrival of new babies in the family or neighborhood, the events of each season in nature and in the lives of their pets, should generally be sufficient to promote a normal and healthy curiosity about reproduction on the vegetable, animal and human levels, so that there will be little need to make special occasions for imparting information about sex to the children.[1]

And if a child, at any stage of his growth has, for one reason or another, developed an abnormal interest in matters of sex, or picked up distorted or inaccurate ideas from playmates and friends, the best means of restoring the balance would seem to be, again, to give him as much accurate information as he really wants, in practical terms of the immediate purpose of the marriage act, the production of a new baby. There are various books on the market written by doctors, in simple language, for mothers expecting their first children. We parents might do well to keep such a book on hand, so that if one of our children needs to study at least a part of such an impersonal, sympathetic and accurate statement of all the stages by which a baby comes into existence, we shall have it ready. And such a book is invaluable for our own use also, to insure that our knowledge of the facts of sex is so clear and correct that we can translate it at need into language that our children can understand.

And beyond the actual physiological facts of sex, we should of course be ready to help the children, during all the stages of their development, to relate their increasing awareness of sex to the great Design of God for mankind. In other ages, parents might have felt with some justice that their whole duty in this matter consisted in imparting the "facts of life" to children in early adolescence, and, perhaps, in

[1] For excellent suggestions as to specific ways of telling children the facts of sex, see *Christopher's Talks to Catholic Parents,* by David Greenstock (Templegate, Springfield, Ill.).

141

giving some additional information on the eve of marriage. We today, however, need to do a great deal more. We need to equip our children, as future apostles and co-workers with Christ, to evaluate and rectify the enormous amount of information and misinformation, of truth intermingled with falsehood, of right attitudes tangled with wrong, which are current in the world today.

It is not possible today for either adolescents or adults to avoid thinking more about sex and its implications—whatever one's vocation—than is, perhaps, normal or ideal. But if our children have been trained to think about it, pray about it, and act about it rightly, that is, in relation to the whole of God's plan and their part in fulfilling that plan, then this modern preoccupation with sex need not harm them. Let us, then, do our part of this training as well as we can, and ask God Himself to make up for our deficiencies, so that our children will grow up and always deserve the Beatitude, "Blessed are the clean of heart, for they shall see God."

d i s c u s s i o n topics

1. What are the practical problems and difficulties of actually giving sex instruction to the individual child? How can parents get over or get around under reticence and other difficulties?

2. What are the sources from which children are most likely to get a false, distorted and unhealthy attitude toward sex? What can be done to offset these forces by a Christian approach to sex?

3. How does the Christian meaning of sex contrast with what the author calls the "fog of Manichaeism," i. e., the idea that sex is shameful and not to be mentioned?

4. Discuss the customs of modern society which raise special problems about sex. What are the wholesome Christian ways in which teenage boys and girls should meet? At what age should "dating" be allowed for girls? boys? Should there be a set hour for returning from a date or a party? Should parents themselves be responsible for chaperoning teenage parties?

5. In what ways can the virtues of purity and modesty be positively developed? What constitutes modesty of dress for girls? What if the styles in formals and swimming suits are of questionable propriety? To what extent is maintaining beauty and dignity and respect toward sex a job for group action by parents?

1. Why has sex become a particular problem in modern society?

2. What were the effects of original sin on God's design for marriage?

3. What positive suggestions does the author make for helping parents to give sex instruction naturally and honestly to their children?

4. What is the true mystery and awe about sex and human reproduction?

5. What advice does the author give for handling cases in which children have an abnormal interest or have picked up distorted ideas regarding sex?

11 attaining our ideals

We have been considering how best to try to bring up our children in accordance with Christian teaching, what lines we should try to follow in training them how to think about and deal with reality. For this purpose, we have been trying to apply the great principle that God Himself uses in teaching us His truth and giving us His life in the Church, the sacramental principle that reality on every level is planned by God to raise our minds and hearts to Himself, and, if rightly used in Christ and for Christ, is meant to be a means whereby we can take our part in building up God's kingdom in love. We have been trying to see how this principle may be applied to the actual facts of daily family life, and to do so in the light of Christian teaching, particularly as shown in the liturgy of the Church and in recent Papal encyclicals.

We have observed that, for most of us at least, the process of trying to give our children a thoroughly Christian education implies, first of all, that we revise and rectify our own ways of thinking and acting. A proverb attributed to the

Jesuits says that nobody really knows a subject until he has taught it; so we parents find that the necessity for teaching our children the art of Christian living almost forces us to try more earnestly to master it ourselves. As parents, we begin to realize how much we need to think about our faith and its implications, how much we need to pray for grace and to try to live fully Christian lives, so that it may be a whole integrated way of life and thought, at least in germ, that we hand on to our children.

In essentials, then, this sacramental way of living and thinking implies that we think of everything dynamically, in terms of the growth and perfecting of Christ's mystical Body, the building up and the victory of His kingdom. We see all history at once as a battle and as a work of construction, the battle of the City of God with the city of the devil, the perfecting of the City of God taking place somehow in and through the battle.

We see also that the life, Passion, Death and Resurrection of our Lord is, so to speak, the main plot or story-line or pattern of this battle as it should be waged in each life, as it is being fought out in the whole history of mankind; that this redemptive work of His is also the pattern for building up His City.

We are preparing our children, then, to become Christ's soldiers and fellow workers, to share in the fellowship of His sufferings with all their work, with all their sufferings, in the joy of His companionship and of the victory that He has already won. We are preparing our children to find and to take whatever special part God made and endowed them to take in this great work.

This purpose implies that the children learn to think about themselves and other people as Christ's members and to treat them accordingly. It implies that they learn to think about all created things as signs of God's truth, as means to His praise and service, as means to serve Him in the loving service of others. This purpose implies that the children learn to see heaven and earth as full of God's glory, that they learn to see their churches as God's special meeting-places with mankind, the gates of heaven, images of the heavenly City.

This purpose implies that the children learn that all human work and human suffering is meant to be a share in Christ's work of building up His kingdom, that Christian play is meant to be a reflection of the effortless activity of Him who is Pure Act, in whose image and likeness we are made. This purpose means that we try so to live that the pattern and framework of our days and weeks and years is, again, the pattern of our Lord's life, Death and Resurrection as the Church shows us how to translate it into daily living.

And this purpose means that we try so to live and act in ordinary family life that—as a shadow exists because of the thing that casts it, as a picture exists to represent some reality, as means exist for the sake of ends—so all our eating and drinking is ordered toward the holy Eucharist and the eternal Feast of heaven; all our building and decorating is ordered to the building-up of God's eternal Temple; all our cleaning and clothing to the preservation and adornment of our Baptismal robes of grace; all our care and training of the children to the shaping of the living stones of the heavenly Jerusalem; all our sleeping and waking to our Lord's Death and Resurrection, to our final awakening with Him to the glory of everlasting life when all things shall have been made new.

Now there are two obvious difficulties to such an application of the principle of sacramental living to ordinary family life today. The first is, how in the world can we parents find time and energy, under modern conditions, even to begin

147

to carry out such a program, to work and play with the children, or even to be with them long enough seriously to train them or to try to influence their outlook and actions?

This difficulty is a very real one, as every parent knows. On the other hand, all authorities agree on the fact that, even under modern conditions, the basic assumptions and tastes and prejudices of a child's own family are still the chief influence in his formation. Willy-nilly, then, we shall hand on to our children to a great extent our own ways of treating people, of acting about possessions and work and the use of time, as well as our standards of taste in home decoration, in food, in literature and so on. And since we cannot help transmitting our standards in some degree, is it not our plain duty to make as sure as we can that these are thoroughly Christian?

But it is also true that most of us could make some time to be with our children, to work and play with them, if we really tried to do so. Here, it would seem, is part of the necessary asceticism of married life: to conserve one's time and strength so as to be able to work at being a parent. Perhaps, for instance, if we went to bed earlier than we have been doing several nights a week, Father would not come home from the office too tired to discuss scouting with big Jimmie or to play with small Peter or read to young Jane; and Mother would not be so completely exhausted by the day's work that she only begins to come alive again after the children are in bed . . .

At least we must always find the time and energy for the greatest necessity of all, that of keeping open the channels of communication with each child during all the years of his growth, by seeming to have time at his disposal, time to listen, time to sympathize, time simply to be with him. For otherwise he will resent whatever preoccupation stands between him and us (and if this be religion, so much the worse for it).

The second difficulty is, perhaps, even greater: Would not children brought up along these lines feel queer, especially with their own contemporaries; would they not grow up maladjusted, misfits for life in today's world; might they not so resent their difference from other people that they would come to hate us and their religion and even, perhaps, leave the Church?

In answer to this difficulty, it must first be acknowledged that if we hope to have our children grow up even as the most minimal sort of Christians, obeying the commandments of God and the Church and keeping out of serious sin, they will have to be and to feel "different" to some extent at least. For we shall have to bring them up to think about and believe many truths that other people do not think about or believe, and we shall have to bring them up to standards of conduct other than those of the majority of their contemporaries.

Since this is so, would it not be better to try to bring them up by one integrated standard of positive Christianity? Would it not be an even greater cause of neurosis or maladjustment to give them, even implicitly, two different standards at once, that of Christ in absolutely vital matters of faith and morals, that of the world in everything else? Perhaps the restlessness, unhappiness, neuroticism of so many Christians today (it is a fact, for example, that an undue proportion of alcoholics are Catholics) is the result of trying to live by such a double standard and to be as much like everybody else as possible, short of actual sin.

In any case, our Lord knew that His followers would have to be different from other people, "If you had been of the world, the world would love its own, but I have chosen you out of the world, therefore the world hates you." If we

149

do everything in our power, then, to help our children to adjust vitally and healthfully to this inevitable difference, rather than trying to minimize it, our Lord will surely help them to grow up without being harmed by it.

How then, can we help our children to make such an adjustment? First of all, let us try to make sure that we ourselves are deeply, habitually convinced of the truth and value and joyfulness of whatever we are consciously trying to influence the children to think or do.

Secondly, let us never insist on more than the Church herself does in the way of Mass attendance, confession, holy Communion, prayers. And let us never use the weapons of ridicule, displeasure, indirect criticism and so on to persuade them towards more than the minimum, but only the positive means of example, peaceful teaching, reasons suited to their understanding. For instance, we ourselves may be most deeply convinced of the desirability of daily Communion, but a child must learn by God's grace to desire It himself; we cannot safely try to impose daily holy Communion on an unwilling child.

Thirdly, let us try as soon as possible to show the children the reasons for what we command, recommend and do, especially when our practice varies from that of our neighbors and contemporaries. And let us never insist on our own whims or strictly personal tastes.

For example, we must insist that our children do not read immoral or realistically violent comics. But we have no right to forbid them to read truly harmless comics on the grounds of poor art or bad taste. We can only try to give the children a taste for real reading, and to show them that much looking at comics is a childish and rather silly way to spend one's time. Let us, in other words, try to enlist their own reason and sense of humor on the side of Christian living from as early an age as possible, but never try to enforce by our authority more than is really necessary.

Again, let us try so to talk and live and act that the children will never have real reason to think that being old-fashioned, dowdy, behind the times, etc., are synonyms for being Christian. We should rather try to show them that to be fully Christian means to be more truly sophisticated, more "hep" than other people can be. To this end, we can try to make sure that all the outward signs of our Christian living, pictures, statues, cards, etc., are as technically good as we can get. No teenager or grown-up is embarrassed, for example, by the presence of a Fra Angelico reproduction in his home (and it is quite possible to obtain such reproductions of masterpieces cheaply) or by a really first-class example of modern religious art; it is the sticky-sweet so-called "popular" and the inane-looking "modern" crucifix or statue whose presence in the family living room makes the sensitive teenager blush.

Again, let us try not to confuse the qualities of Christian child-likeness with childishness, ineptness, or lack of due maturity. We want our children to remain child-like and not to fall victims to the false sophistication of the age. But this cannot be accomplished alone or mainly by negative means. We must rather see to it that our children dress themselves, for example, in accordance with real norms of suitability and taste, modified by current and local fashion. And where, for instance, modesty demands a great variation from the current fashion, let us try to teach them to see for themselves that immodesty is not becoming to anyone and that an immodest dress does not, in actual fact, serve one of a dress' chief purposes, that of helping them to look their best.

Along the same lines, let us try to ensure that the children acquire a reasonable proficiency in whatever sports are played in their neighborhood by children of their age, that they learn as they grow up all the normal social skills, and are not kept away from all means of keeping up on information about ball teams, popular songs, etc. We should try to see to it, for example, that the children acquire a real knowledge of what good swing is, and how to distinguish it from poor jazz; that they know how to dance modern as well as classic and folk dances properly.

To sum all this up, let us not be in any way afraid of any of the manifestations of modern American culture, simply because they are new, different from what we were accustomed to, etc. But let us try, with the help of the Holy Spirit to find whatever is of value in them, and to show the children what this is and how to use it, while rejecting what is wrong and meretricious. Thus they will be on the way to becoming truly sophisticated, men and women of creative Christian taste, ready, if God wills, to help in the formation of a true American Christian culture.

But more than this, let us try to show the children that, as Catholics, God has given them special privileges and responsibilities toward the rest of the world. For no merits of ours or theirs, God has told them more about reality than other people are aware of; God has given them means of dealing with it that other people do not have; God has given them a source of joy and vitality and strength not granted to everyone. And He has done all this so that they will be able to share His truth, His life, His joy with others not so highly privileged.

It may not be at all clear how they can go about such a task when many of their friends and acquaintances seem to know so much more than they do, to be so much more grown-up and sure of themselves perhaps than they. But if they work to appreciate their own great treasures of the Christian faith, and to appreciate the needs of other people rather than thinking about their own deficiencies, God will show them how to be His leaven, His messengers, His co-workers in sharing that treasure with all their neighbors.

Far greater, of course, than the difficulty caused by feeling different from non-Catholics is that caused by feeling different from the good Catholics among whom we may live, who, for one reason or another, have not as yet become aware of the necessity for trying to think out and carry out Christian principles in every field of human life. For if we try to give the children any holier-than-thou feeling of superiority to their fellow-Catholics, we shall only turn them into nasty little prigs, not into apostolic Christians. The solution here would seem to lie in the early enlistment of their own awakening faith, reason, taste, common sense and humor in the battle against being just like everybody else. Would our children really think it better to do exactly what other children are doing? Do they think they would really enjoy it for long? And if so, what other children, since every family differs somewhat both in what is allowed and what is forbidden.

Obviously, whatever we do, the children will rebel often and again against our authority and against any standards we may set. After all, the children would be subject to the effects of original sin even if all the parents around us had exactly the same standards as we. No parent, however lax, seems to be always in good favor with his children! And besides their natural rebellion against our authority, the children will blame us for the struggle in themselves between all kinds of temptations and the habits and standards which we have helped to give them.

This again seems to be an inevitable part of growing up. Do we not remember such rebellion in ourselves? Here, surely, is the place for prayer and great love and sympathy

153

to tide over the complete transfer of authority from us to the children themselves, until they realize fully that the task of becoming Christ's co-workers has become their own responsibility, between them and God, and that we are not going to butt in.

Above all, therefore, we need to remember all during the children's years of training that it is the formation of Christ in each child, the special image of Him that each is meant to become, that is of supreme importance. To have what looks like a "Christian home," to lead an outwardly well-ordered Christian home-life, these are means to the end that the children and ourselves may grow up in all things in Christ.

The value of all external practices, ceremonies, family customs, then, must be judged by the norm of whether or not they really are helping to achieve this purpose. (Here, perhaps, is also an answer to the question of how to introduce older children to the more full, more externally manifested Christian life which their parents have just discovered or are in the process of discovering.) All externals are meant at once to express and foster the reality of Christian living. But any Christian who is old enough to reason and to choose must see the connection between the reality and the external expression we are giving it; otherwise it will neither express that reality for him nor foster it in him. Younger children perceive such connections intuitively; but older children usually need the same kind of patient, rational explanation as do their parents.

For example, small children do not need much talk to grasp the general purpose of an Advent wreath; they like the smell of pine, the special ceremony, and the flame of the candles (especially if they are allowed to take turns at blowing the candles out). And the growing light of each week fits in beautifully with their mounting excitement at the approach of Christmas.

But a teenager might well be desperately embarrassed at the whole idea, especially if it was suddenly introduced into his home. Suppose his friends found him going through all that some evening! An Advent wreath is certainly not an essential part of faith or morals; if an explanation of why we ourselves have come to think that its use is a good way to prepare for our Lord's coming really does not register with a child, it might well be better to give him ungrudging leave to stay away from the whole ceremony. It would be still better, of course, if he and his friends could be made interested in all that such a practice implies, by methods similar to those which awoke our own interest. But if this is not possible, let us try to adhere to the main purpose to which such practices are, after all, only secondary; and look for some other way, more suited to this child, of preparing him for Christ's Christmas coming.

Yet, when all is said and done, the task of bringing up our children as Christians is clearly beyond our own powers. We are only ordinary men and women, not the marvels of sanctity, wisdom, prudence, discretion, charity, and skill that parents obviously ought to be in order to carry out their vocation. Even to bring our children up to be decent human beings usually seems more than we can hope to accomplish! Our strength and comfort, surely, is to realize that the task of training our children is primarily not ours, but God's, and that He is far more interested in the outcome than we. It is He who is in charge of our children's up-bringing; we are only His instruments and deputies.

But, for His own mysterious purposes, He has given us these particular children to bring up for Him. He must, therefore, in some way beyond our understanding, have suited us to them, our special abilities, circumstances, virtues, faults, and defects to their special make-up and their special needs. If we try, then, to serve Him in them with all that we have of intelligence and strength and skill, little as this may seem or may be, we can trust Him to do the rest, to perfect His own Work, so that "doing the truth in charity" we and our children may "grow up in all things in Him who is the Head, that is, Christ."

ᴅ ɪ s c u s s ɪ o n ᴛᴏᴘɪᴄs

1. List suggestions for getting children to participate in religious practices over and above the minimum. Should children be promised secular rewards (going to a movie) for performing a religious act? Should they be threatened with the loss of a secular value (going to a party) unless they perform certain religious counsels (going to daily Mass for the week)?

2. Conduct an experiment in drawing up imaginary schedules in which each family would review the past week and try to see if it would have been possible to increase its religious participation simply by organizing the schedule better. Would it be possible for most families to cut down on the present activities of its various members? Do teenage children today have too many extra-curricular activities? In what way might religious participation help to strengthen the "family circle"?

3. Will the family which follows a pattern of sacramental living necessarily seem "old fashioned" and "behind the times"? Discuss.

4. Discuss the relationship of children to their parents. In the Christian concept of the home will the attitude of the children toward their mother be somewhat different than toward their father? Is it normal that parents should always be in "good favor" and "popular" with their children? Can parents expect to discipline their children and to hold up ideas and standards without the children sometimes resenting or misunderstanding them?

5. Read aloud the final two paragraphs of the chapter. Discuss the role of Divine Providence in our efforts to establish "family-life-in-Christ."

1. What are the two most serious difficulties to the application of principles of sacramental living to ordinary family life?

2. Did Christ expect His followers to be "different"? Explain.

3. Should parents insist that their children do more in way of religious observance than the Church herself commands?

4. Do the obstacles to sacramental living come only from non-Catholics?

5. Should parents expect that their children will be uniformly submissive and agreeable to their plan for sacramental living?